Villains, Victims and Tragedies

Stories from the Dorset Assizes

Brian Bates

*All receipts for this book will be donated to
the Refuge Welfare Committee*

Roving
Press

Step-Up Books

© 2021 Brian Bates

Published by Roving Press Ltd under their Step-Up Books Imprint
4 Southover Cottages, Frampton, Dorset, DT2 9NQ, UK
www.rovingpress.co.uk

Distributed by Brian Bates, 15 Garfield Avenue, Dorchester, Dorset DT1 2EY
Tel: 01305 263824. Email: brianbates@trayfoot.co.uk

The rights of the author to be identified as the Author of this Work have been asserted in accordance with the Copyright, Designs and Patents Act 1988.

First published 2021 by Roving Press Ltd

ISBN: 978-1-906651-374

British Library Cataloguing in Publication Data
A catalogue record for this book is available from the British Library

Front cover photos: *Funeral procession of Joseph Trevitt (courtesy of the Grove Prison Museum). Assize court (courtesy of UCLan Special Collections and Archives, the Livesey Collection).*
Back cover photos: *Gallows (Source: Proceedings of the Dorset Natural History and Archaeological Society. Vol 32). Giving the all clear (© Illustrated London News/ Mary Evans Picture Library). Highway robbery (© Illustrated London News/Mary Evans Picture Library). Child sweep (courtesy of the Wellcome Collection, attribution 4.0 international [CC BY 4.0]).*

Set in 11.5/13 pt Minion by Beamreach Printing (www.beamreachuk.co.uk)
Printed and bound by Henry Ling Ltd, at the Dorset Press, Dorchester, DT1 1HD

Contents

To William Musk
who died tragically aged 20
through no felonious act
5 August 2020.

Acknowledgements

I would like to take this opportunity to thank the people who have helped me produce this book. First and foremost, I must thank by wife Doreen who helped me select the stories for the book and acted as a sounding board for my writing, often coming up with that illusive word I was looking for. Thanks are also due to Karen Tynan who teased out some of the genealogical balls of wool. Several people have been very generous in allowing me to use their resources. In particular, Ann Brown at the Shire Hall Museum, John Hutton, curator of the Grove Prison Museum, Geoff Kirby and David Carter of the Portland Museum, and the staff of the Dorset Museum. Thanks too to Naomi Clifford for allowing me to use images from her excellent book on Maria Glenn, and Sir William Hanham for allowing me to use his family portraits. Jacob Trayfoot also has my thanks for taking some of the photographs in the book. Last and by no means least, thank you Julie and Tim of Roving Press, who through their professionalism turned my imperfect manuscript into this book.

About the Author

Brian Bates and his wife have lived in Dorchester since 1971. His love of social and economic history was ignited by an inspirational schoolmaster and his passion for the history of Dorset began when he wrote a thesis on Dorchester's seventeenth-century history. For him, 'real history' is the story of the ordinary person and their communities. Brian gives talks on various topics, including aspects of Dorchester's and Dorset's rich history. Previous books published include *Dorchester Remembers the Great War*, a tribute to those who are listed on Dorchester's Great War memorial, and *Living with the Enemy: Dorchester's Great War Prison Camp* (both published by Roving Press and available on Amazon). He also transcribed the diary of William Whiteway, a seventeenth-century Dorchester merchant, and has written three military biographies.

A judge of the western circuit. Sir James Alan Park KC (1763–1838), by Henry Edward Dawe (engraver). A.C. Coslett (artist), 1825. (Courtesy of Harvard Law School Library.)

Introduction

My wife and I had lived in Dorchester for just a few months when, one day, I was walking up Grey School Passage towards High West Street. On approaching the junction, I heard the sound of a trumpet fanfare and curious to know what was going on I hastened my pace. Rounding the corner, I saw what I thought was a somewhat strange spectacle. There was a procession making its way up the street. What made it strange to me was that it was led by a man in holy orders, followed by someone dressed in what looked like the naval uniform of an officer from the operetta *HMS Pinafore*. Behind him walked a person in a black tail-coat suit, carrying a black rod, and following him was a begowned and fully wigged judge. These were escorted on each side and behind by a contingent of policemen, and at the rear were several other official looking persons. Enquiring from another spectator as to what was going on, I was told that it was the red judge being escorted to the Crown Court in County Hall, where the assizes were held. I did, of course, know about assize courts but not of this act of pageantry that accompanied them, and certainly not the fact that similar processions had gone on in Dorchester for centuries. Having witnessed this novel event, I put it out of my mind. In the following year, my wife and I were recruited to act as presiding officers in the local elections and were told to report to the Old Crown Court in High West Street for a briefing. As soon as I entered the room it was like walking into history. Other than a change in the colour of the paintwork, it had remained the same since the date the building in which it was located, the Shire Hall, was built in 1797.

It occurred to me then that this must have been the very court in which the Tolpuddle Martyrs, whom I had learned about at school, had been tried and sentenced to transportation to Australia. It was obvious where the judge had sat and where the unfortunate six had stood, and I imagined them being examined and the witnesses giving their evidence and, finally, the terrible verdict. My mind was back in 1834 and I did not hear most of the briefing. Fortunately for the voters of Dorset, my wife did.

While researching my first book I took out a subscription to one of the internet genealogy sites which gave me access to newspapers dating back to the 1700s. Browsing them, I came across reports of assize court cases held in Dorchester during the nineteenth century. Looking at the types of crimes and people involved in them led me to believe that they contained an important aspect of Dorset's, and indeed England's, social history.

This photograph of High East Street was taken around 1860 and shows the Shire Hall in the right foreground. The entrances to the Crown Court can be seen on the right of the photo. When the court was sitting the road was covered with a thick layer of straw to deaden the noise from horses' hooves and cartwheels. (Courtesy of Dorset Museum.)

Examining the assizes of the period not only reveals many fascinating stories but also offers a glimpse of the attitudes of society towards crime and punishment, attitudes that changed over the century. In 1823 the number of crimes that could attract a death sentence was reduced by over one hundred and in 1830 horse stealing and housebreaking were taken off the list. After 1838 only murder, high treason, arson in a royal dockyard and piracy attracted such an extreme punishment. The last public hanging took place in 1868 and in 1861 public whipping was stopped, although it continued behind closed doors until 1948. There were also important changes in the law on the rights of accused persons, but one serious anomaly that remained throughout the century was the lack of legal aid.

In the days before radio, television and mass media, newspapers were the sole method for relaying news to the masses, and when it came to reporting the work of the assize courts reporters were always present while business was being conducted. Some courts, like the one in Dorchester, had a dedicated press box, which might contain several reporters recording proceedings.

The length of the reports of individual cases depended on their importance or local interest. The more interesting trials were recorded in great detail, some taking up three or four columns of a broadsheet newspaper, but in most cases the crime, the name of the accused and the nature of the punishment were all that appeared. Proceedings were recorded in the order they occurred in the court, and remarkably little additional comment was made, except, where appropriate, to point out the novelty, gravity or particular interest of a trial. Occasionally mention was made about the appearance or attitude of a witness, who might be described as 'shabby in appearance' or 'eloquent'. Similarly, observations were sometimes made about prisoners, as in the case of a child who could barely see over the top of the dock, or the extraordinary behaviour of Edwin Preedy.[1]

When it came to the tone of reports, they were decidedly deferential, reflecting the fairness, mercy and quality of British justice. Judges tended to be flattered by being referred to as 'learned' or 'worthy', whilst the convicted might be described as 'wretched' or even 'unfortunate'. Judges were never criticised, but sometimes surprise was expressed at the verdict of a jury. This deferential style of reporting may have been because newspapers did not want to be excluded from the courts, which the judges could easily do. The style of reporting was equally important to the authorities, who wanted to impress the severity of the law on the masses, and doubtless they kept a close eye on what was published; not that newspapers were uncritical of court decisions, particularly in sensitive areas like infanticide and the concealment of a birth, as in the case of Emma Pitt.[2] Such denunciations appeared after the trial and were by no means confined to local newspapers. Neither was sensationalism a characteristic of court reports, though opportunities were taken to introduce a little humour or more flowery language when reporting on what they considered to be a frivolous case, such as breach of promise or bigamy. Sensationalism when it did occur came in the form of broadsheets produced after a trial and sold to the public with headlines like 'Grand Moral Spectacle' and 'House of Murder'.

---

1 See page 156.
2 See page 122.

What court reporters did not realise was that with each stroke of the pen they were painting a picture of contemporary Dorset, seen through the eyes of the court. More significantly perhaps, they also showed how through the microcosm of thousands of individual cases British society was changing during the nineteenth century.

As is so often the case when writing about events that happened in the past, the problem is not what to include but what to leave out. Among the thousands of trials heard throughout the century in Dorchester I have selected what I consider to be some of the most interesting and significant of the period. Most were heard in the criminal court and some were considered quite sensational. Like those nineteenth-century newspaper reports, the stories in this book have not been embellished or sensationalised. The facts have come from the mouths of witnesses, prosecutors, defendants and judges, and any additional observations or comments were those observed in the court. Lastly, a note about the illustrations in this book. Many of them originate from newspapers and books published in the nineteenth century. Consequently, the quality of some of them is not as good as I would have liked.

Background

The Circus Comes to Town

The assizes were held twice a year – at Lent in March, and in the summer in July – and the arrival of the judges in Dorchester was a most impressive affair, as it was meant to be. The authorities wished to impress on everyone the solemnness and importance of the law. The Dorset assize usually followed that of Hampshire, the judges travelling from Winchester to Dorchester by coach, but they were not alone. They were accompanied by carriages packed with assize clerks and barristers, followed by a luggage train and a gaggle of travelling lawyers. When they got to Yellowham Hill, five miles east of the town, the procession was met by the High Sheriff of Dorset and his entourage and the impressive procession continued its journey. The arrival of a judge was an event that the local press were always keen to describe in great detail. On 10 March 1860, for instance, the *Salisbury Journal* reported on one arrival.

'Mr Baron Channell was met by G W Digby, Esq, of Sherborne Castle, the High Sheriff, and the Under Sheriff, T F Fooks Esq, of Sherborne. The High Sheriff was dressed in a plain Court dress, but his equipments were splendid – the coachmen and footmen being in cocked hats, blue coats, scarlet plush knee britches, white silk stockings, and wore shoes with gold buckles. Of javelin men[3] there were 24, in a uniform of blue coat with a scarlet collar, scarlet waistcoat, blue trousers with a small scarlet stripe, and a cockade or rosette of blue, yellow and scarlet ribbon attached to the hat. The liveries were furnished by Mr Arnold, tailor, draper, etc., of Sherborne and Mr Tassell of Dorchester. The carriage was black and yellow, with the High Sheriff's armorial bearings emblazoned on the body in blue and gold. On the hammer-cloth[4] was a gold ostrich. The carriage was drawn by four magnificent greys. The pendents from the trumpeters' instruments were of silk, with the arms of the High Sheriff emblazoned thereon in blue and gold. Altogether the cavalcade was described as the best that has been witnessed in the town for many years.'

---

3   Court officials whose job it was to protect the judges and keep order in the court. They were usually elaborately dressed and carried long javelins.
4   A large decorative piece of cloth placed over and around the seat of the coachman.

The judge's procession arrives at the Shire Hall. The body of javelin men can be seen with their pikes. (Courtesy of Dorset Museum.)

As the cavalcade made its way to the Shire Hall the fanfare of the trumpeters competed with a peel of bells of St Peter's church, rung to advertise the arrival of the judges. In 1851, things changed when, instead of stepping down from a coach, the judges alighted from a railway carriage, at Dorchester South railway station. Their journey was now quicker and more comfortable. Other changes came in 1867 – the javelin men were replaced with policemen, the church bells ceased to ring out their welcome and the trumpeting stopped, an event that the *County Chronicle* commented on when it wrote: 'There seemed to be a general impression amongst the townspeople that the substitution of constables for javelin men was a decided improvement; but, in the absence of the ringing of bells and flourish of trumpets which have hitherto characterised our assize days, the town seemed unusually dull.'[5]

5   *Chronicle* 1/8/1867.

The trumpet fanfare was reintroduced in 1874 after Justice Richard Quain complained that he was not shown enough respect. The chief constable was told to ensure his lordship was not insulted again and had his two trumpeters given some lessons from the bandmaster of the 3rd Dorset Rifle Volunteers.

The shrieval procession, as it was called, was always a popular event for Dorchester folk before the diminution of the ceremony, and a crowd always turned out to see the spectacle, the audience swelled by the large number of visitors who were brought to the town by the assize. As well as jurors and witnesses and court officials, there were friends and relatives of the accused and a large contingent of attorneys and barristers. The *Kentish Gazette* informed its readers that there were no less than sixty barristers at the 1837 Lent assizes for just three cases.[6] The increase of the town's population for a few days each year was of some economic benefit to the town's hoteliers, innkeepers and shopkeepers. Not that the judges would be staying at any

---

6   *Kentish Gazette* 28/3/1837.

of Dorchester's hotels. They had their own lodgings adjoining the Shire Hall[7], where they lived a sumptuous life, with servants and a cook to wait on them, eating the best food and drinking the finest wines. On the evening of their arrival the judges would be entertained to dinner, paid for by the High Sheriff, and occasionally there would be an assize Ball.

After arriving at his lodgings, the first thing on the judge's agenda was to take the 50-m journey to St Peter's church, where, joined by local dignitaries and the usual congregation, a service was held. The High Sheriff's chaplain normally read a sermon which suited the occasion. At the 1874 summer assize he chose his text from St Matthew: 'For there is nothing covered, that shall not be revealed; and hid, that shall not be known.' He then went on to tell those present that this assize was just a faint echo of the Great Assize in heaven when all must render an account of what they have done in the body, and added that justice is frequently miscarried, doubtless something the judge was not too pleased to hear, but at the great judgement day all secrets would be revealed. After the church service it was time to return to the court to begin business.

In the criminal court the first thing to be done was for the clerk to read out the Royal Proclamation against Vice ,[8] while in the Nisi Prius court[9] another judge was preparing to hear the list of civil cases. Next, the grand jury had to be selected and sworn in. The grand jury played a significant part in the criminal process. Its role was to hear the charge against the accused and decide if there was sufficient evidence for the prisoner to be tried by a petty jury. If after reading statements and interviewing witnesses for the prosecution, but not the defence, they felt there was a case, then it was declared a 'true bill'. If not, it was categorised 'ignoramus' and the accused was free. In coming to its decision the grand jury had to be sure that there was a prima facie case to be answered, a point Justice Alderson felt compelled to remind them of in 1831 when he said, 'The true rule, for your guidance, is to find no bill against a man unless you are perfectly satisfied that there will be sufficient evidence against him to enable the petty jury to convict him.'[10] Jurors on the grand jury consisted of county magistrates and were selected by the High Sheriff,

---

7   Originally a separate house, the lodgings were bought by the county in 1827.
8   George lll's Royal Proclamation For the Encouragement of Piety and Virtue, and for the Preventing and Publishing of Vice, Profaneness and Immorality beseeched the people to be against sexually explicit material. It called for the suppression of books and publications dispersing such poison to the young and unwary and to punish the publishers and sellers of such material.
9   The court of Nisi Prius heard civil actions.
10   *Chronicle* 28/7/1831.

but service was not compulsory. However, the job had a degree of prestige attached to it. At the 1831 summer assize twenty-six magistrates answered the call, from which the quorum of twenty-three was chosen. It consisted of some of the most notable landowners in the county, including the families Frampton, Hanham and Moreton-Pitt, plus some members of the clergy. Throughout the century the composition of the grand jury continued to be called socially from the county's elite.

The list of cases to be heard during an assize was called the calendar and the number to be heard varied considerably from one session to another. Invariably, the judges congratulated the grand jury on their law-abiding county when the number was low and commented to the contrary when it was high. In March 1845, for instance, the calendar was particularly high, with seventy-one cases on the list. This prompted Justice Erle to comment on the bad state of crime in the county, but four months later, when there were just thirteen cases, Mr Judge Baron Platt was congratulating them on the diminution of crime in Dorset.

The Crown Court, viewed from the public gallery. (Courtesy of the Shire Hall Historic Courthouse Museum.)

Fortunately, Dorchester's Crown Court still exists in a condition very much the same as it was in the nineteenth century. His lordship the judge sat at one end of the room on a platform under an arched canopy, upon which was painted the royal coat of arms. High up to his right was boxed

One of the cells under the Crown Court. A narrow staircase took the prisoners directly into the dock. (Courtesy of the Shire Hall Historic Courthouse Museum.)

seating for the grand jury, members of which entered via a door which led directly from their room. The small dock where the prisoner stood facing the judge was placed in the middle of the court. No seating was made available, except in rare cases, which meant that in a long trial a prisoner could be standing all day. Prisoners waiting for their case to be heard were kept in cells under the court, with direct access to the dock via a narrow staircase.

Attorneys and barristers were accommodated in the well of the court between the judge and the prisoner, and there was boxed seating on each side of the court for the petty jury, witnesses and the press. Witnesses were usually required to stand whilst giving evidence. As for friends and relatives of the accused, they were accommodated in the public gallery at the back of the court, which meant they could only see the prisoner's back and were therefore unable to give any signs of encouragement or support to them. On days when there were multiple cases to be heard, the court was chaotic, what with the comings and goings of prisoners with their warders, witnesses, attorneys and the public. And of course, it could be a very emotional place. Newspapers reported numerous instances where relatives of condemned men and women broke down in tears or became hysterical when a verdict went against their loved one. Equally, there were instances of amusement and laughter. At the summer assize of 1828 Justice Park was going to stop a prosecution of an alleged horse thief going ahead because of a technicality. The indictment against Robert Foot accused him of stealing a grey mare, but throughout the document the animal was referred to as 'him'. Counsel for the defence explained that in the West Country it was customary to refer to mares as him. He added that, to redress the balance, all tom cats were called she.

The Trial

In 1800, persons accused of a crime and their victims had very different rights and obligations to those of today. In nearly all cases, initiating a prosecution was not the duty of a public body, like today's Crown Prosecution Service, but a private affair. It was up to the injured party to bring a charge, or if that were not practical an interested party would be encouraged to do so. In some instances, people were offered rewards to bring a case against someone.

The normal process for an arrested person was for the accused to be examined summarily by a magistrate or a bench of magistrates, who would decide whether the case could be adjudged there and then or whether it had to be referred to a higher court. Alternatively, the prosecutor could bypass the magistrates' court and go straight to the grand jury for a bill of indictment. By 1850 things had changed, with solicitors and the police becoming more involved in initiating cases, and in 1879 the Department of Prosecutions was established. Coroners' courts also had the power to remit a case to assizes, following an inquest into a suspicious death.

At the beginning of the century trials were not led by counsel but by the judge. Only in government cases of treason and sedition and those involving bank fraud cases was counsel employed. By the end of the century the position had been completely reversed, with nearly all prosecutions being led by counsel. That is, if the accused person had the money to hire one, and most did not. There was no legal aid provision throughout the nineteenth century, except in a few cases where it was provided by a charity.

It was the job of the petty jury to hear the evidence and come to a verdict as to the guilt or innocence of an accused person. The most venerated principle of British justice, since Magna Carta, has been 'the lawful judgement by his peers' as a precondition for a person losing their liberty, but throughout the nineteenth century the composition of petty juries was completely unrepresentative of society as a whole. In 1800, to qualify to serve you had to be a man owning freehold land worth at least ten pounds a year or leasehold land worth twenty pounds a year or occupy a house with fifteen or more windows. One trouble that concerned the minds of the authorities was the poor quality of petty juries. In Dorset, jurors tended to be small farmers or shopkeepers who did not have the necessary education to deal with complicated cases. There was also the problem of independence in a county where the economy was overwhelmingly agricultural and the outlook distinctly feudal. It must have been difficult for a juror who was a farmer to keep an open mind when having to decide on cases of rick burning or the breaking up of machinery during the Swing Riots.[11] Having said that, juries in most cases of poaching, which involved trespass, gave remarkably unbiased verdicts. One area where the law did take social background into account when selecting juries was when the prisoner was a foreigner. In 1846, Pierre Mallet, also known as 'French Peter', was indicted for murder and before the trial began the judge told him that he was entitled to have half of the jury made up of French men. He declined the offer and was found guilty of manslaughter.

Prisoners were at a disadvantage even before they got to the Crown Court. At the summary hearing before the magistrates they would be aware of the charge against them but were not allowed to see the written depositions of witnesses which might be used against them later on. If they were literate they might make a note of the evidence given, but many of the accused were barely able to read or write. At the Lent assize in 1837, for example, of the thirty-one prisoners on trial, one could neither read nor write, twenty-two could read and write imperfectly, and only one could read and write well.[12] The situation regarding witness depositions was largely rectified in 1836 with the passing of the Prisoner's Counsel Act, which allowed the defendant to inspect and copy them.

The majority of accused who were committed to appear at the next assizes were sent to the county gaol to await their trial. For some it meant languishing in prison for up to six months, whilst others had barely enough time to prepare their defence. In 1812, for instance, John Bellingham was tried just three days after he murdered Prime Minister Spencer Percival and was hanged four days after that. Cases themselves rarely lasted more than a day and most were expedited inside an hour. It was estimated that in 1833 the average length of a trial at the Old Bailey was eight to ten minutes. The main reason for this was that the vast majority of cases were undefended.

In Dorchester, when a prisoner was brought up from the cells of the Crown Court and put in the dock the indictment was read out to them, to which a plea of guilty or not guilty was required – a simple thing one would imagine, but this was not always so, especially when the accused was a child. At the 1835 Lent assize, 11-year-old Elizabeth Mellish, described as 'a half-starved

---

11 The Swing Riots of 1830 was an uprising of agricultural labourers in the south and east of England against the use of mechanisation. Destruction of machinery and setting fire to hayricks were forms of retribution against farmers and landowners.
12 *Chronicle* 2/3/1837.

An assize court in action. An intimidating place for most. (Courtesy of UCLan Special Collections and Archives, the Livesey Collection.)

little girl',[13] stood at the bar charged with stealing a hare from a kitchen at Litton Cheney, to which she pleaded guilty. Justice Erle asked her if she knew what she was saying: 'Yes' was her reply. The judge then enquired if she had been visited by anyone in the gaol to discuss her case and, following her negative answer, he told her that she was too young to make a considered judgement and advised her to plead not guilty, which she did.

The prosecution began the legal duel by making a short opening statement to the court and then called its witnesses. At the end of a witness's testimony the defendant or their representative had the opportunity to cross-examine, or the judge might interject at any time with a question. In most cases few defendants were confident enough to cross-examine. It was then time for the defence to make its case. If a person was defending themselves, instead of making a proactive challenge to the accusation they could make an unsworn written statement which was read to the court. The advantage of this was that they did not have to go through the ordeal of cross-examination by the prosecution. Defendants could also call witnesses, either to their character or to fact.

13 *Devizes Gazette* 20/3/1835.

After both sides had been heard the judge gave his summing up to the jury, emphasizing any particular facts pertinent to their decision or any points of law they needed to be aware of. In most instances the jury did not retire but decided on the spot, after conferring. Until 1858, in the event of a jury not being able to come to a verdict, they were locked in a room without fire, food or water until they did. This tactic of starving the jury meant that they rarely failed to come to a verdict. In some cases, if they could not make a decision before the judge was due to leave for the next county it was not unknown for a jury to be put in a cart and follow the judge until they did. If they still had not reached a decision before the county boundary was crossed they were discharged from the cart to find their own way home. After 1858 it became more prevalent for a jury to be discharged and the case retried. The judge was duty bound to accept the verdict, although he might well comment on it. An example of this occurred in a libel case in 1797, when to the astonishment of the court the jury found the defendant not guilty. On the verdict being declared, the judge, Justice Lawrence, replied, 'It is your verdict and not mine'.[14] A judge's own view on the culpability of the convicted person could, however, be expressed in the severity of the sentence he could pass under law. Throughout the nineteenth century those who were convicted and sentenced had no appeal court to go to. Their only hope was to apply for a royal pardon or remittance of their sentence.

Punishment

Throughout the nineteenth century considerable changes were made to the type of punishment given out by the courts. In 1800 there were no less than 222 capital offences punishable by death. They included the most serious offence of murder, down to impersonating a Chelsea pensioner or damaging London Bridge. In Dorset, where the temptations to crime were more rural, stealing of sheep, cattle or horses, and the burning of a hayrick were capital offences. However, in most cases where the ultimate penalty could be applied, death was recorded by the court but was then commuted by the judge to transportation or imprisonment.

Transportation to America was introduced in the early eighteenth century as an alternative to hanging but ceased in 1776 because of the War

---

14   *Chester Chronicle* 15/9/1797.

of Independence. Following the discovery of Australia, transportation was resumed and became the predominant punishment for felons.[15] Over the eighty years of its existence it is estimated that 160,000 women, children and men were transported. Those that behaved during their sentence might be granted a 'ticket of leave'. This entitled them to look for work and live in a particular community until the end of their sentence or until they were pardoned. Those who did not behave themselves were sent to more remote convict colonies, or if they committed another crime they would have their sentence extended.

In 1823 the number of crimes that could attract a death sentence was reduced by over one hundred and in 1830 horse stealing and housebreaking were taken off the list. After 1838 only murder attracted such an extreme punishment. The last public hanging in Britain took place in 1868 and in 1861 public whipping was stopped. Transportation ceased in 1867, when the last transportation ship bound for Van Diemen's Land[16] left British shores the previous year.

As an alternative to transportation the punishment of penal servitude was introduced in 1853, although it was a full fourteen years before it finally replaced it totally. Penal servitude, which was designed both to punish the prisoner and to provide a deterrent to would-be offenders through hard labour, began with a period of solitary confinement, followed, inside the prison, by endless hours on a treadmill or the hand crank, or doing monotonous tasks like picking oakum.[17] The treadmill was a particularly vicious punishment, where men were required to tread on steps attached to a revolving barrel, the equivalent to walking upstairs. In effect, it was no better than veiled torture. In the 1860s a scientific committee concluded that the distance a convict could be required to ascend was 8,640 ft per day. Outside the prison, convicts would be sent to do public works, like roadbuilding or quarrying, and in 1848 the first specialist public works prison was built on Portland.

Portland prison was established as a temporary measure to house convicts building a breakwater to provide shelter for shipping. In 1867 the government declared that it would remain open, providing hard labour by employing men in the stone quarries.

---

15 Someone who committed a serious crime.
16 Van Diemen's Land, the original European name for the Island of Tasmania, contained one of the largest convict colonies.
17 Prisoners were given lengths of rope which they had to unravel into individual fibres.

Convicts being searched after working in the quarries. (Courtesy of The Grove Prison Museum.)

It was not long before the prison gained a reputation for its harshness and brutality. Up to 1,500 convicts were accommodated in individual cells measuring just 4 ft by 7 ft.

Brutality took place on both sides, with several warders being injured or killed.[18] The favourite way of punishing the prisoners was by flogging them with the cat-of-nine

Conditions in the prison were harsh. This cell, c 1849, was just 7 ft long, 4 ft wide and 7 ft high. The walls were lined with corrugated iron and hot air was fed in from a central boiler. Convicts ate in their cells and slept in hammocks. (Courtesy of the Grove Prison Museum.)

18   See the stories of Edwin Preedy (page 150) and Jonah Detheridge (page 118).

tails, and those who were deemed to be too weak to undertake this terrible ordeal were put on bread and water. It sometimes took several warders to lash a prisoner to the frame for his whipping, and his cries could be heard outside the prison. The combination of unhealthy conditions, poor diet and brutal treatment resulted in a high number of deaths. Eventually news got out that prisoner deaths were occurring at almost one a week, which caused public concern to the extent that questions were asked in Parliament. One judge was reported as saying that had he known the conditions in the prison he would not have passed some of the sentences he had, but it was not until 1897 that the Director of Prisons admitted that the punishments on Portland were worse than any other prison.

Portland prison was a popular tourist attraction. (Courtesy of Portland Museum.)

From its inception the prison became quite a tourist attraction, and some locals offered guided tours whilst others converted the upstairs rooms of their houses into tearooms, so that customers could watch the convicts working in the quarries. In 1921 the building was converted into a borstal and today it is a prison and Young Offender Institution.

The County Gaol

In 1305 Edward I granted a petition from the people of Dorset to build, at their own expense, a prison at Dorchester and to detain there persons indicted for trespass and felony. This event is remembered on a plaque attached to a building on the corner of High East Street and Icen Way which claims to be the site of the first county gaol. Those condemned to death had

John Speed's 1610 map showing the gibbet (fig. A). The original gaol was sited at the junction of Gaol Lane and High East Street (fig. B). The site was then moved to the bottom of High East Street (fig. C), before the existing prison was built on the site of Dorchester Castle (fig. D). (Source: The Municipal Records of the Borough of Dorchester, C H Mayo).

but a short journey down Gaol Lane and Bell Street[19] before arriving at the gibbet on Gallows Hill.[20]

On route to their fate the convicted were given the opportunity to have a last drink at the Bell Inn before meeting their end. Rev. Richard Cutler[21] tells the story of one unfortunate man who refused his last glass of refreshment and went straight to the gallows, and just as the cart he was standing on drew away someone rushed up with a pardon. The rope was cut but all the attending surgeon could do was declare 'Too late!'

Both these buildings served as the county gaol, on the same site at the bottom of High East Street. The style of the carriage in the illustration on the left suggests that that building may have been the one that replaced the other in 1624. (Courtesy of Dorset Museum.)

At some time in its history the site of the gaol was moved to the eastern extremity of the town, just inside the Roman east gate. We do not know how many times the building was modified or rebuilt, but William Whiteway, a Dorchester merchant, tells us in his diary that it was rebuilt in 1624.[22] In the seventeenth century the prisoners held there were those who were waiting to appear at the assizes or those awaiting execution. Towns in the county had their own houses of correction and bridewells (gaols) for their own miscreants. When the new gaol was built, a local man, Robert Cheeke,[23] was asked to come up with some significant wording to be put on a plaque to be placed above the prison entrance. From then on, any unfortunate prisoner entering the gaol would be greeted with the message 'Look to yourself,

---

19   Icen Way was originally divided into three parts: Icen Way, Bell Street and Gaol Lane.
20   Gallows Hill is now part of South Walks.
21   See Cutler.
22   See Whiteway.
23   Robert Cheeke (1572–1617) was the headmaster of Dorchester Free School.

this is the scope. Sin brings prison, prison the rope.'[24] We know that those incarcerated were allowed to entertain visitors and some had their wives staying with them. The new prison was nonetheless a formidable place. An inventory of the time contains implements such as hand bolts, cross-bolt fetters and a terrible sounding instrument called the tailor's shears.

In about 1700 the gallows was moved to a site between the Roman amphitheatre and Weymouth Road on the southern edge of the town.

The gallows by the Roman amphitheatre. Originally it was placed inside but moved because of erosion of the walls, caused by the crowds attending executions. (Source: Proceedings of the Dorset Natural History and Archaeological Society, Vol32.)

When a new gaol was built in 1795, hangings took place over the outer entrance of the prison, facing North Square, and by 1858 the site had again been moved; then hangings took place over the main door of the building, overlooking the water meadows. The last public hanging in Dorset was held in 1863[25], after which executions took place inside the prison grounds. The last execution took place in Dorchester in 1887.

For nineteenth-century inmates, the new prison life was just as punitive as ever, even if the technology had changed. Prisoners were still put in irons and fetters, added to which there were the obligatory treadmill and crank machine for those undertaking hard labour. There was never a shortage of inmates in the gaol and in 1848 magistrates were discussing whether it needed enlarging. They were told that the building could accommodate 140 prisoners, with only eight single cells for women and

---

24   See Underdown.
25   See the stories of Fooks and Preedy (see pages 203 and 150).

three for solitary confinement; for men there were 119 single cells and ten for solitary confinement. Rev. Templar contended that such overcrowding led to better-disposed persons being 'contaminated' by others.[26] He gave one example of where a girl who had stolen turnips was sharing a cell with one of the worst prostitutes in Weymouth. The chairman, Rev. Yeatman, said that one of the main problems occurred at night, when the next morning evidence had been found of crimes being committed 'of a most revolting nature'.

Not all inmates of the prison were associated with Dorset crime. Some were there because of their conscience. One such person was Gilbert Wakefield,[27] who spent two years in the gaol, convicted of seditious libel. He was a vociferous critic of the government and declared that the poor and the labouring classes would lose nothing if the French invaded. During his incarceration, his family lived in Dorchester and visited him regularly. Gilbert spent much of his time helping poorer prisoners.

Richard Carlile was another man of conscience, who was said to be the most important campaigner for freedom in the first half of the nineteenth century. Born in 1790, he gained employment as a tinsmith and in 1813 married Jane, who bore him five children, three of whom survived into adulthood. It was when he got into financial difficulty after his employer arbitrarily reduced his hours of work that he began to get interested in political reform. Carlile had always wanted to earn his living with the pen and began writing to the newspapers and corresponded with radical agitators like William Cobbett[28] and Henry Hunt[29]. In 1817 Carlile was earning his living by going around the streets of London selling pamphlets and journals of political reformers. He then decided to rent a shop in Fleet Street and became a publisher, reprinting the works of people like Thomas Paine[30]and William Hone[31]. For the latter's works he was imprisoned for four months, for seditious libel and blasphemy.

Carlile was convinced of the power of the written word and fought

---

26   *Sherborne Mercury* 1/7/1848.
27   Gilbert Wakefield (1756–1801) left Dorchester prison in May 1801 and died four months later.
28   William Cobbett (1763–1835), radical politician and pamphleteer who pushed for parliamentary reform.
29   Henry Hunt (1773–1835), radical activist and major influence on the Chartist movement. He spent two years in Dorchester gaol as a result of his part in what was later to be called the Peterloo Massacre.
30   Thomas Paine (1737–1809), English-born American political activist and revolutionary, arrested several times for his beliefs.
31   William Hone (1780–1842), writer and satirist, and a champion of free speech.

vociferously for the freedom of the press and became one of the leading voices on radical thought, advocating universal suffrage and the establishment of a republic. These were dangerous views at the time, and he realised that he was likely to lose his freedom again, but he was quite willing to go to prison for his beliefs. He was indeed arrested again, in October 1819, for publishing the works of Thomas Paine. His punishment was to spend six years in Dorchester gaol and pay a fine of £1,500, an enormous sum at the time. If the authorities thought that imprisoning Carlile would bring an end to his writing and publishing, they were very wrong, for it was inside Dorchester gaol that he did some of his most significant work. He had his favourite writing desk brought into his cell and managed to get the authorities to agree to numerous visits from his friends and wife Jane, who took over publishing his pamphlets and his newspaper, *The Republican.* His life of imprisonment in the county gaol was luxurious compared to the rest of the inmates:

> 'Carlile's room was large, light and airy. It had a sink, water-pipe, and complete lavatory attached, the necessary outfit being provided for hot and cold water at pleasure. A sofa was also supplied. Every other consideration was shown as regards the prisoner's physical comfort. In this respect Dorchester Gaol was far superior to most of our "reformed prisons" of today. … He was not allowed to make the acquaintance of any other of the inmates of the prison. To this end, he was closely confined to his room.'[32]

Carlile's solitary confinement ended when his wife joined him in 1821, after she and his sister, Mary Ann, had been convicted of seditious libel. Jane was sentenced to two years imprisonment and Mary Ann to one year, also to be spent in Dorchester. Husband and wife shared the same cell and while they were together another child was born.

Such was the dislike of Carlile in many quarters that fellow radical Francis Place felt compelled to warn him not to eat any food in the prison he had not prepared himself or that had not been prepared in his presence, after hearing stories that an attempt would be made to poison him. Carlile had a generally good opinion of his time in Dorchester gaol, but it was tainted by his encounters with his gaoler, whom he loathed. In one letter he described the gaoler as 'the greatest ruffian I ever saw in any kind of office'[33], and in another, written after his release, he told Rev. Robert Taylor, who was in gaol

---

32   See Aldred.
33   Letter dated 11/10/1825, quoted in Campbell.

for blasphemy, 'Blaguard, vile and wicked as was that gaoler, I made him fear me, simply by looking at him. Yet I never expressed myself toward him that he could describe it as an insult or a threat; I conquered him by my virtue.'[34] The gaoler appears to have had equal respect for his special prisoner. Having returned from London where he collected the warrant for Carlile's release, he went into his cell and declared, 'Now I have your discharge, and the sooner the better.'[35]

Carlile was released in November 1825 and continued with his calling. He was again put in gaol, not Dorchester, for two and a half years for writing an article in support of agricultural labourers campaigning against wage cuts and advising strikers to regard the government as their enemy. During the latter part of his life he lived in extreme poverty and died in 1843, leaving his body to medical science.

Of course, there were the inevitable escapes from the gaol. An amusing incident occurred in December 1847 when the landlord of the Castle Inn on Portland received a letter from the Governor of the gaol offering a reward of two pounds for the apprehension of a man named Puckett who had escaped. From the description the landlord was sure that someone drinking in the tap room was the very fellow. After talking to him he was sure; but what to do next? More in hope than expectation, he ordered a carriage and pair and somehow managed to persuade Puckett to hop in. To his surprise he did, and they set off for Dorchester. It was not long before Puckett was back safely in his cell.

Dorchester prison continued to house prisoners into the twenty-first century. At the time of its closure in January 2014 it was accommodating 252 male inmates, about half of whom were on remand. It had served the county of Dorset for 209 years.

---

34   Ibid.
35   See Campbell.

The Judges

Assize court trials were held by the most senior judges in the land. 'The Twelve', as they were known, were recruited from persons practicing at the bar. Most were appointed by the Lord Chancellor and there was no retirement age. In society they enjoyed considerable prestige, their names were well known, and their work was reported widely by the newspapers. These were the leading advocates and needed to be well educated to deal with the complicated cases that came before them. More than a third of them appointed during the century had a first-class university degree and many wrote scholarly texts on the law. Not only did the judges interpret and enforce the law, but also they created it through their decisions, establishing case law, and there were instances where the verdict of a judge was thought to be a major influence on changing statute law made by Parliament. For instance, Sir William Maule was considered by his colleagues to be an excellent judge who combined common sense with legal knowledge and was affectionately remembered for his irony. At the Warwick assizes, Maule sentenced a financially poor man to a day in prison after being convicted of bigamy, after his first wife had deserted him and lived with another man. The judge then went on to outline at length the various legal steps that would have to be taken in order to obtain a divorce at the prohibitive cost of about £1,000. Maule's decision was said at the time to have contributed to the change in social opinion which led to the 1857 Divorce Act.

An important part of a judge's job was to address the grand jury, called the Charge. During the Charge, the judge directed the jury's attention to the more difficult cases on the list, explaining points of law or fact. He also took the opportunity to explain any changes in legislation that would affect their decisions as jurors or their role as magistrates. Some judges also used the occasion to make what some regarded as a political speech. In 1843 Justice Atcherly reminded the members of the grand jury of their responsibilities to the poor[36], and in 1839 Judge Erskine gave his views on the importance of education, particularly religious education, in reducing crime.

As powerful and venerated as they might be, judges were also human beings, with the foibles that went with it. Justice James Willes was well known for crying during trials. On Boxing Day 1856 a child died of convulsions after being fed with laudanum in its bottle. Willes was brought

---

36   See page 116.

to tears several times during the evidence, especially when details of the child's death were given. He reportedly buried his face in his notes and could barely continue with the trial. Other judges seemed to take delight in reprimanding the jury when they thought they had come to a wrong verdict. Lord Alexander Cockburn had a reputation as a Casanova. Taking advantage of being away on circuit, he often took his wife with him, but, as someone pointed out, each time he did so it was a different Lady Cockburn.

The aforementioned Justice Maule was practical as well as witty. During one session in Lincoln, on a hot summer day he ordered the staff in the court to smash the windows instead of going onto the roof to open them.

Sir Alexander Cockburn (1802–1880). A brilliant judge who became Lord Chief Justice and had a reputation as a Casanova. (Source: Caricature drawn by Carlo Pellegrini, which appeared in Vanity Fair in 1869.)

Poaching

Serjeant[37] Atcherly, presiding over the Crown Court at the Lent assizes in 1843 described the crime committed by the men standing before him as one of the most outrageous he had ever known. The four prisoners, Edmund Hounsell, James Brake, Samuel Bowditch and Edmund Hounsell (Junior), were charged with 'having, together with many others to the number of six or more, in the night, at the parish of Whitchurch Canonicorum, armed with guns and other weapons, unlawfully entered certain enclosed lands of the Right Hon. Lord Bridport, for the purpose of taking game'.[38]

Twenty-two-year-old John Richmond knew the area around the village of Whitchurch Canonicorum intimately. Not only did he live there with his parents, but also he was employed as a gamekeeper by Lord Bridport. He also knew of a gang of poachers known as the Milton Men, so called because they came from West Milton, part of the parish of Powerstock in West Dorset. On the night of 23 November, previous, John was out with several other men, searching for poachers. They had just reached an area known as Rough Close when gunshots were heard, coming from a nearby coppice which was used for the raising of pheasants. John sent his brother and another man to one part of the coppice, whilst he and Joseph Collier went to another. Stealthily, John approached the wood, and just as they reached the edge of it seven men emerged not ten yards from them. Among those he recognised were Samuel Bowditch and James Brake, two of the Milton Men, both of whom were carrying guns. The other poachers were variously armed with guns, pistols, and sticks. It was one of the gang who spoke first, as John approached, within fifteen yards of him. The man threatened, 'Stand you b_____ [sic], or else I'll put a ball through you'. John replied, 'You won't do that I suppose', which prompted the response, 'Damn my eyes if I don't', and the poacher walked towards the young gamekeeper, pointing the muzzle of his gun at him. At that point, undeterred, John raised his gun to his shoulder and told the man that if he lived long enough he would pay him the same compliment. The gamekeeper then lowered his firearm and went among the gang, who had been watching the drama, but as he got there a threat came from another man that he would shoot him. Realising the perilous situation that he was in, John summoned help with a whistle and, as his colleagues approached, the

---

37   Serjeants-at-Law were barristers who were members of an order of the English bar. The term was abolished in 1875.
38   *Sherborne Mercury* 11/3/1843.

Like smuggling, poaching could be a violent business. Here, two gamekeepers are being attacked by poachers. (Source: Archive.org.)

gang began to leave, walking across a field, followed by the gamekeepers. At some stage the poachers stopped and John once again went among them; this time one of them threatened 'Damn and blast your eyes, if you don't go I'll blow your brains out'.[39] But, instead of leaving, John walked over to a bag he had spotted which contained pheasants, and as he bent down to pick it up he was stopped by a blow to the side of his head which knocked him to the ground.

This act prompted four other members of the gang to set on Joseph Collier, beating him to the floor with the butts of their guns. The assault only stopped when John regained his senses, picked up his gun and approached them, at which point the assailants retreated up a lane, followed by the keepers at a safe distance. Realising that they were not going to shake off their pursuers, the gang tried throwing stones, which did not deter their followers, so they decided to stand their ground, again threatening to shoot the men if they did not leave them alone. Then, after a shout of 'Shoot the b_____' [sic] from someone, a gun was fired, resulting in some shot hitting John near his eye and temple and some going through his hat. Another gun was fired, causing one of the keepers, a farmer named Copp, to exclaim, 'Oh dear, I have been shot in the leg'. Realising what they had done the poachers then made a speedy escape. Fortunately, the wounds inflicted on the two keepers were not fatal and both men recovered.

The fact that some of the poachers had been recognised meant that it was not long before the police were rounding them up. PC William Lee had the

---

39 Ibid.

job of arresting them. Brake and the younger Hounsell were detained in Wyke Regis, near Weymouth, whilst the constable had to make a journey to Jersey where the older Hounsell had fled in the knowledge that the arresting authorities would have to apply to the governor of the island for his release.

Defending the four men in the dock, Mr Wilde gave what a newspaper reporter described as a very ingenious and eloquent address to the jury, advocating that there was little evidence to identify the prisoners. Eloquent or not, it did not convince the jury, who returned a verdict of guilty. The judge indicated his view of the seriousness of the case by sentencing all the prisoners to seven years transportation.

The convicted man James Brake was more easily recognisable than the other poachers despite the darkness of the night. The 37-year-old, who was a married man with three children, was only 5 ft 3½ in tall and had prominent cuts on his temple and the bridge of his nose. Neither was it the first time he had been convicted of an offence. At the age of 22 he appeared at the Quarter Sessions for not providing sureties after being convicted of bastardy and spent a few months in prison. Shortly after his conviction in the Crown Court James was transferred to the prison hulk *Stirling Castle*,[40] moored off Devonport, to await transportation, but there is no record of him ever leaving British shores. It is not clear whether he remained on the ship or went on to a shore-based prison, until he received a pardon on 10 March 1847.

The same path was followed by Edmund Hounsell (Senior), who accompanied Brake to the *Stirling Castle*. Up to 450 men were crammed onto the ship and the conditions were appalling. Dr Risk, a medical officer working on the vessel, told an investigating board looking into prison ship conditions, that diseases common among the convicts on the hulk were tuberculosis, scrofula and bowel complaints, not surprising when one imagines the damp environment in which they lived and the unwholesome food. A typical diet for the men consisted of a weekly ration of biscuits and pea soup, accompanied once a week by half an ox cheek and twice a week by porridge and a lump of bread and cheese. Dr Risk's conclusion on the diseases he had highlighted was that the best treatment for them was a well-regulated generous diet, pure air, and moderate exercise, all of which were absent on the *Stirling Castle*. Quarterly prison reports indicate that throughout his imprisonment Edmund's behaviour was good, which doubtless contributed to his early release on 9 December 1847.

40   The *Stirling Castle* was a 74-gun third rate ship of the line launched in 1811 at Rochester. She served as a prison hulk from 1835 until 1855.

Of course, it was not only the convicted who were punished for their crime. Time and time again, a man's family was plunged into poverty with the disappearance of the breadwinner. Such was the case of Edmund's wife Susanna, who found herself, together with her eight children, aged between twelve years and two months, a pawn in an argument between Weymouth Borough and the parish of Powerstock, about who should be responsible for paying poor relief to the family. After his release, Edmund returned to Susanna and in 1861 they were living on Portland, where he was working as a sawyer.

The youngest of the four was Edmund Hounsell (Junior), aged twenty-four and nephew of the senior Edmund. He was unmarried and lived with his parents in Wyke Regis, where he earned his living as a fisherman. After the trial he was removed from Dorchester gaol and sent with Samuel Bowditch to Pentonville prison in London. Bowditch, a year older than Edmund, was a married man with one child. The two of them spent ten months in Pentonville before boarding the *Sir George Seymour* sailing for Van Diemen's Land.

Edmund junior's parents, John and Mary, were aged 45 and 55, at a time when the average life expectancy for a woman was 42 and for a man 40, and were devastated by the thought of not seeing their son again, even if he returned after the completion of his sentence. Accordingly, whilst Edmund was in Pentonville they petitioned Sir James Graham, the Home Secretary, asking if his sentence could be served in the UK. The heart-rending appeal, signed by the parents and some local men, read as follows:

'Edmund Hounsell – petition to The Right Honourable Sir James Graham, Bart. MP. Secretary of State for the Home Department.

The humble petition of John and Mary Hounsell of Wyke Regis, in the County of Dorset.

Most humbly sheweth, that your Petitioners' son Edmund Hounsell, was tried at the Lent assizes, 1843, at Dorchester in the County of Dorset, for an offence against the game laws, when he with three others were convicted to transportation for seven years.

That the said Edmund Hounsell is now and has been since the 18th April 1843, confined in Pentonville Prison, London.

That your petitioners are informed that early in the ensuing month their son will be sent to Van Diemen's Land. Your Petitioners, in consequence of their age, have every reason to fear that should such an event take place they shall never see their son again. They, therefore, humbly crave leave earnestly to Petition that this part of his punishment may be remitted and that he might be allowed to serve out the remainder of his punishment in England.

Your Petitioners are the more emboldened by the fact that this was his first offence, that in the assault which took place on the 22nd Nov 1842, he struck no blow, threw no stone, or was in possession of or fired a gun, which is proved by the evidence, his only crime being that he was in company. Up to that time he honestly gained his living by fishing and never was before a Magistrate for any offence or had complaint lodged against him till this occurrence, when, unfortunately, he was led away by old offenders.

Your petitioners also have reason to hope that his conduct during the period he has been in Pentonville Prison will plead in his behalf. Your petitioners again implore your favourable answer to this humble Petition, as they also fear should he go abroad the good he has already received in prison by education and trade will be lost, and your Petitioners as in duty bound will ever pray.

Landowners and inhabitants of Wyke Regis join in the above Petition. – R H Swaffield : Chas Buxton : Thos Hare : Richard Hillary : John Kempsell : William Talbot.'[41]

The reply was curt and to the point: 'Refused application'.

Instead of landing Samuel and Edmund on Van Diemen's Land, the *Stirling Castle* sailed on to Port Phillip, near Melbourne, where they disembarked. Unfortunately, there are few records of their life in Australia, but we do know that they were pardoned. An edition of the *New South Wales Gazette*, dated 28 February 1848, lists pardons granted to convicts the previous July, and among the names are those of Edmund and Samuel. Their pardon was on condition that they did not return to England. The 15 April 1858 edition of the same newspaper had an entry in its unclaimed post column indicating that there were letters which needed to be collected from the General Post Office, in Melbourne, by a Samuel Bowditch living in Brisbane, and another newspaper, named *Queensland's Early Pioneers* and dated 25 November 1858, notified its readers of the christening of a Samuel Bowditch, indicating, perhaps, that Bowditch had married.

***

---

41   Home Office: Criminal Entry Books. Entry Books of out-letters, warrants and pardons, 1782–1871 (NA HO13).

One person who was not in the dock at the trial was John Hounsell, brother to the senior Edmund Hounsell. It is not clear whether he was with the gang on the night in question, but he was arrested and committed to prison until the grand jury determined that there was no bill against him. John had managed to escape justice on this occasion, and it was not the first time. In fact, he had the distinction of appearing before the assizes on three previous occasions and twice walking away, despite the evidence being against him.

The first episode began in 1839 with Rev. George Cookson, clerk in holy orders at St Mary's church, Powerstock, who felt more than a little uneasy about a burial that had taken place in his churchyard the previous November. The deceased was a woman named Mary Hounsell, aged thirty-five, wife of John Hounsell. It may have been the circumstances of her death which aroused his suspicions or the behaviour of her husband afterwards, but whatever his motivation George decided to take the matter further with two Bridport magistrates, who, after hearing what the reverend gentleman had to say, concluded that there was sufficient reason to refer the matter to John Frampton, one of the Dorset coroners. Frampton's preliminary enquiries led him to order that two bodies be exhumed, those of Mary Hounsell and that of James Gale[42] who had died the previous January.

What was described by the *Sherborne Mercury* as 'A respectable jury, chiefly obtained from the surrounding parishes'[43] had the gruesome task of inspecting the bodies the next morning, after which the coroner directed no less than five surgeons to carry out post-mortems. This took the rest of the day, at the end of which the medical men went off to analyse their findings, and as a result Frampton issued warrants for the apprehension of John Hounsell and Elizabeth Gale, wife of James Gale. Hounsell was committed to Dorchester Gaol on 21 March, but there is no record of Elizabeth entering the prison.

When the inquest reassembled the doctors gave their findings on the body of Mary Hounsell, which resulted in the jury deciding that her husband was guilty of wilful murder and, accordingly, John remained in prison to await trial at the next assizes. The inquest into Mary's death had been a marathon, taking nine days, each one lasting between twelve and fourteen hours. The inquiry into James Gale's death was somewhat shorter, the doctors deciding that he had died of natural causes.

Standing at 5ft 4½ in tall, John Hounsell presented a diminutive figure standing in the dock in Dorchester Crown Court before Justice Irvine, who

---

42 Brother of Bartholomew Gale. See page 38.
43 *Sherborne Mercury* 29/7/1839.

had already advised the grand jury of the complexity of the case. Hounsell was indicted for the wilful murder of his wife, at Powerstock, by administering to her a quantity of arsenic. The prosecution's case relied heavily on medical evidence, but first it had to establish that the body exhumed was that of Mary Hounsell. This was accomplished through the testimony of the verger of St Mary's who confirmed that although the body he saw in the church was badly decomposed he recognised it as that of the woman in question.

Main witness for the prosecution was Dr William Herapath,[44] an eminent analytical chemist. He told the court that his examination of the body and the results of extensive analysis led him to conclude that there was not the slightest doubt of the presence of arsenic, and that the amount found in the stomach had led to the woman's demise.

After the conclusion of the medical evidence, Elizabeth Gale came back into the story, called as a witness. She attested that she was a widow who knew the prisoner and his wife. She had been sent for by a local lad, presumably at the instigation of John, and attended Mary Hounsell when she was ill, staying with her overnight on occasions, until she died. During that period, of about two weeks, Elizabeth had made and given her food and drink, and made up a concoction to make her sweat, based on beer, all of which made her violently sick, as did the castor oil bought by John Hounsell, and medicines prescribed by doctors. The witness then informed the court that the prisoner had sent her on one occasion to Mr Roper, a Bridport druggist, who sold her a packet containing some white powder, which she put in her pocket. On her way home the packet broke and a little of the powder was spilled in her pocket, into which she later put some pears, which she ate and was violently sick. The jury must have been surprised, if not shocked, at what Elizabeth said next. That just after her husband's death she had been intimate with the prisoner and about two weeks after that Hounsell had taken her to Radipole and proposed marriage, which she accepted, and banns had been read. Ironically, they were read by Rev. Cookson who instigated the proceedings leading to the trial.

John Hounsell did not give evidence, but a statement was read out to the court on his behalf in which he claimed that he was in the habit of curing cattle and helping people who had the itch, for which, in both cases, he used arsenic. In his address to the jury, defending counsel argued that his client had never denied buying the poison, but there was not a shred of evidence

---

44   William Herapath (1796–1868) inherited his father's brewing business but soon gave it up in order to study chemistry. He was one of the founders of the Chemical Society of London and became professor of chemistry and toxicology at the Bristol Medical School.

that he administered it to his wife. After the judge's summing up, the jury immediately brought in a verdict of not guilty and John was a free man. John Hounsell had avoided imprisonment or even death, but it would not be long before he found himself facing justice again.

***

The first truly modern census in England was held in June 1841 and Charles Pouncy was the enumerator responsible for collecting the names of people in St Peter's parish, Dorchester. Among the places he had to visit was Dorchester prison, and among the names of the 148 prisoners he recorded were those of brothers John and Edmund Hounsell and George Biles, indicted for the crime of being armed with guns for the purpose of poaching and wounding Richard Critchell with intent to murder him. The three men were part of a gang of poachers out on the night of 13 November at Litton Cheney, near Bridport. They were hunting for pheasants, and out hunting for them, on that same night, was gamekeeper Richard Critchell, with a number of helpers. At about midnight, some shots were heard coming from the direction of Ox Copse, so Richard made his way there. Coming to a fence he proceeded to climb it when he heard someone say, 'Put it into him', followed by the firing of a gun, which led to him being wounded in the leg. Meanwhile, elsewhere in the copse, keeper Joseph Salisbury with some of his companions came across another group of poachers, some of whom had guns. Joseph said to them, 'We suppose you won't fire at us,'[45] to which the answer was a volley of gunfire. Richard Critchell was hit on his thumb and some of the other keepers were also wounded, but not seriously.

One witness, Joseph Legg, who admitted to the court that he had been one of the gang that night, gave the names of the others present and specified those who had been carrying guns. He confessed to seeing some of the shooting but declared he could not see who fired, even though it was a brilliant moonlit night. In fact, nobody present could put a name to those who pulled the trigger, but did that matter? According to the law it did not. Justice Erskine told the jury that when several persons were engaged in an unlawful enterprise, each of them was responsible for the events that might ensue. If the jury were satisfied that one of the party had fired a gun, and it

---

45   *Chronicle* 11/3/1841.

was fired for a common purpose, then they must come to the conclusion that all in the party were as guilty as the man who pulled the trigger. After deliberating for a few minutes, the foreman of the jury said, 'We find that they were there for an unlawful presence,'[46] a verdict he could not accept. He informed them that they were required to find the prisoners guilty or not guilty of the charges in the indictment, and after further consultation a verdict of not guilty was declared.

In normal circumstances the vindicated men would have walked out of the court and gone back to their families, but it was not to be. Instead, they were escorted back to prison; they had another appointment with Justice Erskine the following day, where they were to be tried for the poaching element of the events on 13 November. The evidence of the previous day was reiterated and this time the three were found guilty. The judge addressed the prisoners at some length, telling them that he had the power to transport them for fourteen years for such a serious crime, but on this occasion he would not, in the hope that they would learn from their lesson. Instead, he sentenced each of them to a year in prison with hard labour.

The *Chronicle* could not resist commenting on the case involving the shot keeper, particularly on the fact that the person firing the gun was just five yards from his victim. Someone signing himself 'Auditor' wrote the following doggerel:

> A man that can think, by so firing a gun
> That no harm at all was meant to be done,
> Gives pretty clear proof – the contents of his head
> Like those of the gun, were made up of lead.

Edmund Hounsell had no intention of giving up poaching. In 1858 he was again tried at the assizes with shooting Charles Gill, a keeper, with intent to do him grievous bodily harm. He was found not guilty because the gun he fired was not loaded properly, but he was sent to prison for six months for assault.

***

---

46   Ibid.

There are numerous examples of poachers assaulting gamekeepers, but occasionally the boot was on the other foot. Edward Matthews, a sergeant in the militia, claimed that on 15 February 1859 he was walking home from his work with a friend, Alfred Maidment, when they heard a rabbit screeching on the other side of a hedge. They went to investigate and found that a stoat had caught one. The stoat ran off and Edward put the rabbit in his pocket and took some younger ones from a hole. He and his friend then heard someone coming and went to make off, but before they had taken more than a few steps a cry rang out behind them. It was George Trowbridge, keeper to Lord Portman, who warned them, 'If you don't stop, I'm damned if I don't shoot you'.[47] This was followed by a shot into Matthews' back. He fell senseless to the ground with 280 pellets in his body, though was not killed. Trowbridge was immediately contrite and ran up to Maidment and said that he did not know that his gun was loaded and had slipped, adding that he would not have had it happen for five pounds. Maidment told him that he must have known it was loaded and that it was no accident. He claimed that neither he nor Matthews were carrying sticks or nets with them, although it was found that some of the rabbit holes in the area had been freshly dug and some had nets over them. He also admitted that he had been fined in the past for fishing in a pond belonging to Lord Portman, although there was no notice forbidding it, nor indicating its ownership. The judge took a dim view of this, suggesting that it should be reported to Lord Portman and that the person who had Maidment arrested on that occasion should lose two weeks wages. Matthews also admitted that he had spent eleven months in prison for receiving money knowing it to be stolen.

The defence's main line of argument was that the whole thing had been an accident and several witnesses were paraded before the court attesting to Trowbridge's good character. One witness said that he had seen Maidment throw two rabbits over the hedge. Neither the jury nor the Judge, Justice George Bramwell, were impressed. The jury found the defendant guilty of shooting Matthews with intent to cause grievous bodily harm. Bramwell deferred sentence until the following day because he wanted to think things over and, the next morning, before sentencing, he spoke to the prisoner who still professed his innocence. The judge told him that Matthews and Maidment were damaged characters, who had previously been convicted of poaching, and that he had never known a poacher to be an honest man. Whilst he had no love of poachers, there was no reason to shoot them for a couple of rabbits, and they should know that outrageous as they may be, the law would protect them. He declared that the crime committed by Trowbridge's actions was very mischievous and very cruel, just for stealing a couple of rabbits. Bramwell was obviously much affected by the crime, declaring that he deferred judgement because he wanted to take time for any improper feelings he had against the convicted man to dissipate, and after consulting his fellow judge he concluded that the appropriate sentence was four years imprisonment with hard labour. Trowbridge served his time in Chatham and Woking prisons. While her husband was in prison his wife Charlotte remained in the family home in Shaftesbury, and when he was released he returned to her and set up a business as an upholsterer.

Your Money or Your Life

By the beginning of the nineteenth century there was a network of turnpike roads connecting the main towns of Dorset, most of which had been built in the 1750s and the 1760s. They were maintained and administered by trusts set up by acts of parliament, and like today's toll motorways anyone who wanted to use them was required to pay a fee to travel along a particular stretch of the road. At strategic points toll houses were built, with gates stretching across the road, which were opened by a toll house keeper, letting the traveller through after paying his dues.

Whilst toll roads replaced what were previously bad roads, often a quagmire of mud in the winter and full of rock-hard ruts in the summer, they were not universally popular and being a toll house keeper could be a dangerous occupation. Some gates were torn down because people resented having to pay to travel along a highway that had previously been free. Some of the toll houses, like the one at Toller Down Gate between Dorchester and Crewkerne,[48] were in isolated rural areas and could be easy pickings for robbers and thieves.

On the night of 18 February 1846, George Lane, the toll house keeper at Toller Down, was woken from his sleep by a cry of 'Gate', indicating that someone wanted to pass through. He got up and going through the outer door he was immediately set upon by two men, whilst two others went into the house. Lane was held on the floor by one man and was told that they would cut his head off if he did not remain quiet. In the meantime, Mrs Lane, who had heard the commotion, was coming downstairs when she was met by a man wearing a mask and with a blackened face. He knocked her down and said that she would lose her life if she did not tell them where the money was kept. She said that the takings were gone but there was some money on the window sill in her bedroom. The man in the mask held her whilst another went to search the bedroom and found one pound and ten pence, which the gang escaped with.

Neither George Lane nor his wife recognised any of the gang, so a reward was offered for any information leading to the arrest of the culprits. Nothing happened for seven months and then an article appeared in the *Chronicle* informing its readers that a man named Bartholomew Gale,[49] who had been

---

48   Toller Down Gate toll house was located on what is now the junction of the A356 and the B3163, 14 miles north-west of Dorchester.
49   Bartholomew Gale was the brother of James Gale, mentioned in the case of John Hounsell.

working at Grove Buildings in Dorchester, had been arrested by Constable Newman in the Castle Inn,[50] 'after a desperate struggle',[51] on suspicion of taking part in the robbery. In the same month another man, William Reid, was arrested, this time in Bridport. The two men were brought before the magistrates and were committed to appear at the next assizes.

The newspaper did not say what led the police to the two men, but it may well have been information given by the wife of the gang member who held down George Lane. She appeared as a main witness for the prosecution in the trial of Gale and Reid at the 1847 Lent assizes. She claimed that at about 9 o'clock on the evening of the robbery Gale and Reid had been seen talking about the best way to disguise themselves and that her husband told them that a good way would be to tie a handkerchief round their faces and wear a cap. He then gave Gale one of his children's caps to wear, and after blackening their faces with soot from the chimney, Gale, William Reid, his brother John, and the woman's husband left with a lantern. The husband did not return until 6 o'clock the next morning. The witness then told the court that when she spoke to her husband about the robbery he told her that whilst he was holding down Lane, the gate keeper had told him that it was a shocking thing and that they must soon meet their judgement at the seat of Christ.

The only defence offered, by Mr Edwards who represented the two prisoners, was that the jury could place no credit on the evidence of the female witness. Gale and Reid were found guilty and sentenced each to fourteen years transportation. This was the second time that Gale had found himself in the dock of the court. In 1843 he was found innocent of stealing some sheep leather.

Bartholomew Gale, who seemed to be the ringleader of the gang, was born in Powerstock in West Dorset in 1811 and became a shoemaker. In 1837 he married Mary Clarke in the village of Whitchurch Canonicorum, situated about 5 miles west-north-west of Bridport, but she died in childbirth and left Bartholomew with a son. Had she lived she would have received some notoriety in 1856 as the sister of Martha, who was hanged in that year for killing her husband.[52] Bartholomew married for a second time, in July 1846, to Ann Lock who had four children but had never been married. Ann lived

---

See page 32.

50   The Castle Inn was situated halfway down The Grove and is used currently as a fitness centre.

51   *Chronicle* 5/11/1846.

52   See page 59.

in Grove Buildings, West Fordington. For Ann, the marriage would prove to be a short one.

After the trial Bartholomew Gale and William Reid were sent to Millbank prison in London to begin their sentence, and on 30 September 1848 the Home Secretary directed Captain Murdoch of the ship *Eden* to accompany 237 convicts to Australia. Bartholomew was among 203 who had been granted a conditional pardon providing that they did not return home. The ship left Plymouth on 5 October 1848 and 122 days later arrived at its destination. The 24 convicts who had to serve their sentence were dropped off in Van Diemen's Land, but Bartholomew and the remainder of the human cargo continued to Port Phillip near Melbourne. From there he was taken to Geelong, 45 miles south-west of Melbourne. Bartholomew was what was termed an Exile, a prisoner who had served the first part of his sentence back home, the first eighteen months of which was spent in solitary confinement, followed by a period of hard labour. Once he had landed, Bartholomew was, ironically, termed a free man and it would not have been long before he found some kind of employment, perhaps with one of the squatters, who were always looking for cheap labour. The remainder of his life is a blank book, but the one fact we do know about him is that he died on 6 January 1893 at Hamilton Hospital in Victoria, aged 82, and may well have had a better life than if he had remained in England.

William Reid spent longer in England, serving in Millbank, Wakefield and possibly Portland prisons before boarding the ship *Hashemy* in July 1850. In the October he disembarked at Freemantle, Western Australia to start his new life, and it sounds as if it was a good one. In 1851 he was given a ticket of leave[53] followed by a pardon in 1854 and went on to become a landowner and owner of the Yiapa mine. In September 1866 he married Sarrah Sherry in Yandanooka, Western Australia and he died at his farm in 1883, aged 65, leaving behind Sarrah and their six children, plus of course his family back in England. Intriguingly, one of the executors of William's will was a William Gale, which raises the question of whether Bartholomew Gale married again and had a child.

As for Bartholomew's wife Ann, now with a new baby born just after her husband was convicted, the future must have looked bleak. With no income and mouths to feed she now had to turn to the parish for financial help and when she did so the question arose as to which parish should pay to keep the family alive. Under the rules of the Poor Law it was the parish of her

---

53   A parole document showing that the convict could be trusted.

husband's birth that was responsible for supporting her, and an order was made for their removal to Powerstock. Whether she went there or not we do not know, but the 1851 census shows her back in Grove Buildings living as a servant with coal porter Daniel West, whom she married in 1854. As to what happened to the other two men concerned in the robbery, it remains a mystery. They do not appear in the Dorchester Gaol register of admissions, suggesting that if they appeared before a magistrate they were not, for some reason, committed for trial.

***

The enduring image of the highway robber is personified by the likes of Dick Turpin and Jack Shepherd, holding up stagecoaches with the threatening question of 'Stand and deliver; your money or your life?' But whilst such men and women existed, their crime had all but disappeared by the beginning of the nineteenth century and from then on stagecoaches could travel without fear of being robbed. There were several reasons for this. Firstly, the establishment of the Bow Street Horse Patrol meant that roads around London were now policed; secondly, local magistrates were refusing to licence inns and hostels from which highwaymen operated. But, probably the most significant factor was the growth of the banking system, which meant that it was no longer necessary to travel with large sums of money.

Thieves and robbers are nothing if not adaptable and they soon changed their modus operandi to suit the new circumstances. During the period 1820 to 1880 about thirty cases of what were termed highway robberies were tried at the Dorset assizes. In the summer assize of 1835, for example, of the seven cases to be tried, four were for highway robbery, which provoked comment from the judge, Justice Coleridge. When addressing the grand jury, he said, 'These offences on nearly every calendar bear a disproportionate number; and it is lamentable to think that our public ways should become less secure than they were formerly. There is also a peculiar feature about most of these cases which would bring down on the prisoners, on conviction, a very severe measure of punishment; there is in most of them considerable violence, and it appears to be general practice to knock down the victim at once by one single blow, that he might be stunned and unable to recognise by whom he

When the robbing of coaches became less attractive, criminals took to a new form of highway robbery. (Copyright Illustrated London News/Mary Evans Picture Library.)

was assaulted.'[54] As was the case with the earlier form of the crime, they were mostly brutal, cowardly and today we would call them muggings.

There were plenty of opportunities for a robber to pick out a victim in rural Dorset, where agricultural fairs and market days were numerous. Events like Woodbury fair at Bere Regis attracted hundreds of visitors, including farmers who sold their stock there. And, when business was completed, they made their way home with a pocket full of money and often a belly full of beer.

William Orchard was a farmer from the Isle of Wight who formerly lived at Broadwey, between Dorchester and Weymouth. In October 1860 he returned to his home county on business at Dorchester Fair, where he bought some farm implements from a Mr Winzar. At the end of the day, instead of staying in Dorchester before returning to the Isle of Wight, he intended to sleep at Broadwey that night. It was agreed that he would set off on the seven-mile journey on foot and Winzar would catch him up with his cart and take him to his destination.

54   *Chronicle* 23/7/1835.

William told an assize court jury what happened next. Before beginning his journey, he dined at the Royal Oak, in High West Street and then had a gin and water at the Phoenix, in High East Street. On route to Broadwey he popped into the Junction Hotel in Great Western Road for a glass of ale, before setting off once again. In his pocket was his knitted purse containing nineteen pounds ten shillings in gold and fifteen shillings in silver. William only reached the first milestone on Weymouth Avenue when he was pounced upon, pulled

The Royal Oak, Dorchester, where William Orchard dined just before his fateful journey. (Author copyright.)

backwards, kicked, and knelt on, whilst his purse was taken from his pocket. As his three attackers left, he saw the faces of two of them and recognised them as the men standing in the dock, Robert Clifford and John Williams. He lay in the road for about ten minutes, when Winzar came along and took him back to Dorchester on his cart. At the police station William gave descriptions of the men, who, he said, were well dressed, of a navvy-like appearance and not very tall. It did not take long for the local police to arrest two men for the crime, and a few days later William visited Dorchester prison where he recognised 42-year-old Robert Clifford through a window and 27-year-old John Williams from a group of prisoners exercising in the yard.

Sergeant Vickery of the Dorset constabulary described the arrest of the accused, who also included Mary Ann Williams, wife of John Williams. She stood accused of 'Harbouring and maintaining John Williams and Robert Clifford, knowing them to have committed a felony'. Following information received, Vickery and Superintendent Brown went to Wareham, where they believed the suspects were staying at the Lord Nelson public house in North Street. Going into an upstairs room, they found Williams in one bed with his wife and Clifford in another. Williams jumped up and asked what was up, and when told that they were wanted for highway robbery near Dorchester Clifford replied, 'All right, come on Williams', and added, '[If] You prefer a charge against me it's our duty to prove our innocence'. When asked for his name and address Williams refused to give either, as did Clifford, claiming sarcastically that he had lost them some time ago. The two policemen then searched the room and found between the mattress and the bed in which Williams had been sleeping with his wife a purse and a dirty white handkerchief, both containing money. The two men were brought back to Dorchester and remanded. No action was taken against the wife at that stage, but it was not the end of her participation in the story. A few days after the men had been remanded, Sgt Vickery was standing outside the Town Hall in Wareham when Mary Ann walked up to him, called him aside and said she could prove that her husband and Clifford had been wrongly charged – that Orchard had not been robbed by a man at all but by a woman, and to prove it she offered to show him the victim's purse, and they made off to the Duke of Wellington public house. There they discussed the matter over two pennyworth of gin, but no purse was produced. At the trial, mention must have been made of the possibility of a woman committing the robbery because Orchard, when being questioned, took great pains to assure the jury that he was not in the company of a woman that day and that he never went up a lane with one.

Several witnesses were called by the prosecution to support its case, their evidence giving the tale the colour of a Sherlock Holmes mystery. Thomas Gregg, owner of the Great Western Hotel, located in Great Western Road, attested that on the day of the robbery the prisoners came into his yard in a horse and trap and asked for the horse to be stabled there overnight. Clifford also asked for a room, but Williams and his wife went for lodgings elsewhere. After Clifford retired for the night, a stranger with sandy whiskers came to the hotel and asked to see the two men but was told they were not there. The next morning, he returned for a bundle which they had left for him. Seeking lodgings was not easy on that day because of the fair. Mary Garrett was standing by her door when Williams and his wife approached her and asked if she could recommend somewhere to lodge. She said that her son, who lived next door, would put them up. Mary then described how after the couple had retired for the night the wife came down and gave her something wrapped in a handkerchief and asked her to lock it away somewhere safe. She said that she would, but did not, and when she later opened the parcel, she found that it contained eleven sovereigns and three half-sovereigns. As Mrs Williams was leaving the next morning, she asked Mary for the handkerchief and left with the money.

Mr Cole, for the defence, addressed the jury, arguing that there were no suspicious circumstances concerning the money found under the bed. It was merely put there for safety. After all, he continued, public houses are full of all sorts of characters. Furthermore, if they had committed the robbery surely they would not have slept in Dorchester that night but made their getaway. As regards the tale Mrs Williams had told Sgt Vickery about the purse, he suggested that she did it to divert blame away from the two men. His last argument was simply that it was a case of mistaken identity.

In his summing up, Mr Baron Martin told the jury that there was no charge against Mrs Williams because, in law, anything she did was under coercion from her husband. The jury immediately found Clifford and Williams guilty, a verdict the judge concurred with, saying that he had no doubt that they had come to Dorchester that day to rob someone. Each man was sentenced to fifteen years penal servitude. As the two were led from the court they protested their innocence. The men were sent to Millbank prison and a year later boarded the prison ship *Norwood* bound for Western Australia. As to what happened to the man with the ginger whiskers, it remains a mystery.

***

One of the 1835 assize cases involved a poor lad of sixteen, who was terrorised on the road going east from Yeovil to Nether Compton. Henry Phelps had been sent on his journey by his employer, a Mr Jordan, with whom he lived. He had only got about a mile from his house when he was stopped by two men. Henry said that each of his assailants put a pistol to his head and gave him the choice of handing over his money or losing his life. The lad searched his pockets and offered them three halfpence, a comb, and a knife. Not satisfied with the pittance on view, one of the attackers said that he would be damned if he would have that but would have Henry's life instead. At this point the boy decided not to wait around and took to his heels. One of the two men was arrested for the crime – his name William Wotton, a 22-year-old from Whitechapel in London. The Dorchester prison admission and discharge register recorded that he was a single man who worked as a baker, and in appearance he was 5 ft 5¼ in tall, with light brown hair and a sallow complexion, with a couple of burn scars on his face. The record also indicates the punishment he was given: fourteen years transportation.

After a short time in Dorchester gaol Wotton was sent to the prison hulk *York*,[55] anchored in Gosport harbour, before joining 280 other convicts on the prison ship *Recovery*, bound for New South Wales. The *Recovery*'s surgeon recorded some interesting facts about the beginning of the voyage.

'On 5th October 1835, the guard embarked at Deptford, consisting of 1 staff officer, 1 subaltern, two sergeants, one drummer, and 26 rank and file of the 28th Regiment, accompanied by 8 women and 4 children. On the 19th, at Spithead, we received on board 160 male convicts from the Leviathan and 120 from the York hulk, and on the 30th got under way, previous to which, the convicts had to be temporarily discharged to the hulks in consequence of there being a great nuisance on board.'[56]

Wotton spent his time in New South Wales at Liverpool Plains,[57] a large agricultural area, and in 1848 he was granted a certificate of leave, which allowed him to work for himself, provided he remained in a specific area, reported regularly to the authorities and attended church on the Sabbath. As for Henry Phelps, he later married and worked in Yeovil's primary industry at that time, making gloves.

***

The 23 November 1853 was a busy day for William Hyman, waiter at the Ox Inn in Shaftesbury, as was every November when the Shaftesbury Fair was held. On this particular day, some customers drew his attention. The first was a very attractive woman drinking at the bar with two men. The second was a man sitting at a table drinking on his own. He was George Hatcher, aged 42, who farmed and dealt in cattle at Kings Mills, Marnhull. The *Chronicle* described him as 'A large and powerful man but illustrating the easy going and simple-minded qualities more strikingly embodied in our ideas of the British farmer of fifty years ago than the eminent agriculturalist

---

55   *HMS York* was a 74-gun third rate ship of the line launched in Rotherhithe in 1807. It became a prison ship, housing 500 prisoners in 1820, and was taken out of service in 1948 when a serious rebellion broke out.
56   See Neill.
57   Wotton would have known about the terrible event that occurred at Liverpool Plains in 1838. Known as the Myall Creek Massacre, seven convicts and settlers were hanged for murdering thirty aboriginal men, women and children.

of the present day. He was also, though extensively engaged in business, an illiterate man.'[58] Later in the evening the two men at the bar left the woman alone and at about 9 pm Hatcher got up to leave. As he reached the porch the woman approached him, enquired as to where he was headed and asked for a lift. 'You are kindly welcome'[59] was his reply. William Gatehouse, an ostler[60], was asked to bring Hatcher's gig round and he witnessed the couple driving off. On a couple of occasions, the ostler noticed the two men who had been with the woman hanging around and now he saw them set off in the same direction as the gig.

Hatcher had not gone far with his passenger when he heard a man's voice cry out from the darkness, 'Halloo! Is that you? I know you.' The gig came to a halt and Hatcher held out his hand, thinking it to be a friend. He was immediately pulled down and fell into the road, landing on his head. His attacker jumped on him, whilst the woman leapt from the gig and started to rifle his pockets, containing thirty shillings in gold and cheques to the value of £400. After the victim's pockets had been emptied the man holding him tried to get away, but Hatcher was not going to give up without a fight and grasping his assailant around the waist he had no intention of letting him go. Fortunately, a 16-year-old Shaftesbury lad who had also been to the fair was attracted to the scene by a cry of 'Murder!' and when he arrived there he recognised Hatcher as someone he was acquainted with. As he watched the two men struggling he heard Hatcher say to the other man, 'If you will let me up I will treat you to some brandy and water', an offer the assailant declined. Hatcher also said to the woman that she could have the money but please leave the cheques, which were later found in the gig. By now several others had arrived on the scene and with their help the attacker was restrained and eventually arrested.

The trial of the two thieves, George and Ann Taylor, occurred before Mr Baron Martin at the next Lent assizes. Neither had they money to hire counsel to act for them, nor were they entitled to free legal representation, although Ann Taylor did attempt to alleviate the situation. When arrested a watch had been confiscated from her which was not related to the crime, so she asked the judge if she could have it back so that she could use it for hiring an attorney. Judge Martin agreed that the watch should be returned to her but said it was too late in the proceedings to hire a lawyer. Their only option was to defend themselves.

---

58 *Chronicle* 16/3/1854.
59 Ibid.
60 Someone who looks after the horses at an inn.

George Taylor cross-examined his accuser and then addressed the jury in a long, rambling but eloquent speech. After referring to Pontius Pilate, Jesus Christ and Sir Walter Raleigh, he urged the twelve men not to believe anything that was not reasonable and common sense. Having informed them of their judicial obligations he then went on to show, with what the attending newspaper reporter described as 'the utmost plausibility and artfulness',[61] that he was activated by the natural feelings of a man sensibly alive to the preservation of his wife's honour when he saw her driving away from the inn with Hatcher, and when he chased after them he was confronted with the scene of Hatcher and his wife out of the gig in a suspicious attitude. Naturally, he said, his outraged feeling did not permit him to witness anything more, so he jumped on Hatcher. He attempted to convince the jury of the probability of his story, referring to the fact that Hatcher offered him a glass of brandy and water if he would let him go.

Ann Taylor's appeal to the jury carefully followed the line of her husband's. Trying to discredit Hatcher she said that he had made improper overtures to her. Indeed, she assured them that he had spent some time with her in the bar and had treated her to some peppermint and some cakes. According to her he also said that he could give her a bed for the night, and nobody would know, and that he would give her a sovereign in the morning.

There were clearly two very different stories of what happened on the night of the Shaftesbury Fair, but what sealed the fate of the Taylors in the end was a single sheet of paper. Because Hatcher was illiterate, he had asked a friend to write down what he had bought at the fair, with the prices, and this was found on Ann Taylor after she was arrested. It took less than five minutes to find the prisoners guilty. In his summing-up Judge Martin said that it was clear that the two of them had conspired to rob that night with violence, before sentencing George Taylor to seven years penal servitude and his wife to six months imprisonment with hard labour. It is interesting how, unlike in the previous story, Ann Taylor was given a prison sentence because of her positive role in the crime and not considered to be under the coercion of her husband.

Before his conviction Taylor was incarcerated in a prison ward[62] where 'moderate' conversation was allowed, in the continuous presence of an officer, but after being convicted the rules were stricter. He was held in a ward with a separate compartment where he was under constant supervision of a warder and not allowed to speak. When it came to his behaviour, this

61   *Salisbury Journal* 18/3/1854.
62   'Ward' probably meant cell.

was described as 'very good indeed'. When it was time for him to move, a transfer card was made out which gave some details about him. It shows that he was a 30-year-old baker who, for some reason, declared that he was single, so perhaps he and Ann were not married. Intriguingly, though, when he was asked to state his next of kin the record shows that 'He declined to say anything about this'. On 3 July 1855 he was sent to the prison ship *Defence*,[63] moored at Woolwich, before being transferred to Northampton prison to serve out his time.

∗∗∗

Of course, not all assaults on the highway were motivated by money. In all too many cases it was drink that so often led to tragedy, and such was the case near Corfe Castle, in 1834. On Thursday 23 April, Edward Dean, a Dorset coroner, made his way to the cottage of Cassandra Studley[64] in the village of Stoborough, a mile south of Wareham. His purpose was to hold an inquest on the body of William Hall. The *Sherborne Mercury* reported how, 'After a week of intense suffering, this unfortunate person breathed his last, from the effects of the wound received on the previous Saturday',[65] and went on to say that his death had been caused by a shot from the pistol of Isaac Brake, who the coroner's jury found had a case of wilful murder to answer for. He was charged to appear before the magistrates, who concurred with the coroner's court and committed him to Dorchester gaol pending his appearance at the next assizes.

The trial took place in July, where Brake was charged with 'feloniously and maliciously, with a pistol loaded with powder and ball, shooting at William Hall, of Corfe Castle, butcher, with intent to murder him, or to do him some grievous bodily harm'.[66] Several witnesses were called by the prosecution who one by one gave their version of the incident which occurred on the road from Stoborough to Corfe Castle.

Cassandra Studley attested that she and her husband were returning home after visiting Wareham market, when she noticed the prisoner, the deceased, another man and a woman, together in the road. The deceased

---

63 *Defence* was a 74-gun third rate ship of the line. Built in 1815 it was accidently destroyed by fire in 1857.
64 The name is misspelled Stoodly in newspaper reports.
65 *Sherborne Mercury* 28/4/1834.
66 *Chronicle* 24/7/1834.

was leading his horse which then got away from him, and as it did so he shouted to Cassandra to stop it, which her husband did. When the deceased and the accused came to her, she noticed that Hall was decidedly tipsy, but the prisoner Brake appeared sober. Brake immediately got onto the horse and Hall told him that he could not ride it but added that the lady who was accompanying them could. At first, the prisoner took no notice but then dismounted and there then ensued an argument between the two men, Hall saying, 'Go before or after me and don't aggravate me so', and then hitting Brake, not very hard, on the shoulder a couple of times with a small stick he had with him. Hall then grabbed Brake by the coat and noticed that he was carrying a pistol, upon which Brake took the firearm out of his pocket and attempted to cock it, provoking Hall to knock it out of his hand. Brake picked up the gun and fired at a distance of about two yards. Hall immediately cried out, 'The villain has shot me through the loins',[67] and staggered towards the shocked Cassandra and dropped in front of her. It was all too much for the lady's husband who promptly fainted. Brake's reaction was somewhat different. According to witnesses, he very deliberately took a bullet from his pocket, nipped off the paper with his teeth and reloaded his gun, with little concern about what had just happened. He then picked up his bundle and continued his journey. Cassandra called after him that he had shot a man and should come back, but he said that he would not, waved his stick in the air, laughed and walked on. Two men who had heard the shot were George Norris and Thomas Hatchard, who came to Cassandra's assistance. When they arrived on the scene, they found Hall writhing in agony and when Hatchard unbuttoned the man's waistcoat he saw blood on his shirt and a hole in his side the size of a bullet. In fact, the ball had caused terrible injuries. Hatchard picked up the mortally wounded man and carried him on his shoulders back to Cassandra's cottage. Then, Norris and Hatchard set off after Brake who was heading for Kimmeridge, where he worked as a preventative officer. They caught up with him about half a mile from where Hall had been shot. Hatchard asked him what authority he had for shooting a man, to which he replied that as a King's Man he had authority to deal with any man in a similar way who molested him on the King's highway. The two men then returned to the scene of the crime.

Robert Taylor, who was Corfe Castle's postmaster, would certainly have known William Hall and he took it upon himself to go to Kimmeridge to

---

67   Ibid.

seek out the assailant. Like Hatchard, he confronted him about what he had done and received a sharp rebuff, Brake saying that if any person were to molest him as Hall had done he would shoot him, words which he would later regret saying. Taylor next found Mr Cooper, the parish tithingman,[68] who took Brake to the preventative service Station House where the senior officer Lt Carr told Brake to give up his arms, which consisted of a loaded pistol, a swordstick, powder cartridges and five balls. Carr later explained to the court that he had told Brake that it was necessary to carry arms, especially between Stoborough and the Station House, because seizures of contraband had been made there through the vigilance of the prisoner and there were fears of reprisals. Eventually, some constables arrived to take Brake to the police station in Wareham where word had got around about what had happened, and when the party arrived in South Street there was an angry crowd awaiting them, quite happy to lynch the prisoner and save the taxpayer the expense of a trial.

When it came to Brake's defence the best his counsel could do was to introduce an element of provocation on Hall's part and parade a number of character witnesses before the jury. A boatman, named George Vance, claimed that Hall wished to quarrel with him just before the shooting, using offensive and indecent language. Lt Carr attested that Brake did not have a short temper and was particularly mild.

Justice Paterson, in summing up, explained carefully to the jury the difference between murder and manslaughter, and told them that if they believed that the prisoner had shot the deceased, not from malice but from heat of blood caused by provocation, then that would reduce the crime to manslaughter. It took the jury but a few moments to find Brake guilty of manslaughter.

It was when his lordship was passing sentence that Brake's words to Robert Taylor came back to haunt him. The judge recognised that there appeared to be some prevarication on Hall's part, but the crime was so close to murder that it demanded a severe punishment, especially as the prisoner had entertained the idea of shooting anyone who molested him. He would, therefore, be transported for the term of his natural life.

So, it was back to Dorchester gaol for Brake until the authorities determined the path his fate would take him on. An attempt was made to mitigate the sentence when a petition, signed by Sir John Byng, MP for Poole, was sent to the Home Secretary, but was turned down. Brake

---

68   A parish officer responsible for order, particularly at church services.

was sent initially to the prison hulk *Leviathan*,[69] anchored in Portsmouth harbour, where he arrived on 28 August. He was there until 13 November, after which he joined the convict ship *Waterloo*, bound for Australia. Among the 224 convicts on board was another Dorset man, John Long, who had likewise received a life sentence for stealing a purse containing eighty sovereigns. After three months the *Waterloo* sailed into Hobart, the main port of Van Diemen's Land.[70] Brake was to spend nineteen years there before he died, aged 43. After five years of serving his term he made a statement about the circumstances of the shooting. He claimed that it was an accident, and that his pistol went off when Hall tried to take it from him. During his whole time of imprisonment, he received good reports about his behaviour, except on one occasion when he was given six months hard labour. Unfortunately, we do not know what his misdemeanour was. Back in Dorset, it was not only the convict's parents John and Sarah who were grieving for the loss of their son. William Hall's widow Harriet gave birth to a baby girl, named Fanny, a week after her husband's death. Far from being a moment of joy it only added to her burden of having to raise seven children by herself. Somehow, perhaps through the thriftiness of her husband or with the help of friends or relatives, she stayed in Corfe and successfully raised her children on her own, never remarrying. The 1841 census shows her still living in the village, employed as a dressmaker, and the 1851 census records that she was living in East Street, with just Fanny. Sometime during the 1860s Harriet moved to London with Fanny, lodging with a family in Jubilee Road, Chelsea. Fate had dealt her a terrible hand that April day in 1834, but she appears to have made a success of her life despite all the odds against her.

---

69   Launched in 1790, *Leviathan* saw action at the Battle of Trafalgar and became a prison ship in 1818. It was sold out of service in 1848 after being used as a naval target.
70   Known since 1856 as Tasmania.

The Queen's Highway

Being a coach or carriage passenger in the nineteenth century could be dangerous, to say the least. In one column of the *Sherborne Mercury* in September 1845,[71] two accidents are mentioned. In the first, Joseph Ash, a passenger sitting on the outside of the *Magnet* coach, fell off at Puddletown after falling asleep. He broke his leg and was taken to Dorset County Hospital 'In a precarious state'. In the second, someone was killed in what today would be considered a case of reckless driving. Following an inquest in the board room of the County Hospital, coroner John Wallis issued a warrant for the committal of Thomas Margrie, after a jury had found a verdict of manslaughter against him.

The story began in Bridport, when a four-wheeled carriage set off from there to go to Poole, where Louisa Lawrence lived. The other passengers were Anne Weaver, Louisa's niece, and Thomas Margrie, who was driving, his wife Elizabeth, and their three children. At Margrie's trial at the 1846 Lent assizes, Anne Weaver testified that the party left Bridport at 7 am at a gallop, Margrie occasionally using the whip on the horse. Already a little anxious at the speed they were going, Louisa and Anne became frightened and voiced their anxiety by screaming. They told Margrie that he must slow down, which he promised he would and blamed the excessive speed on poor breeching of the horse.[72] After stopping to replace a shoe on the horse at Winterbourne Abbas, they reached the Phoenix Inn in Dorchester at about midday, where his wife told him that he was likely to cause an accident if he carried on driving so fast. Apparently taking little notice of his wife, Margrie again set off at a very fast rate, to the alarm of his passengers. It was when they reached Yellowham Hill near Puddletown that the ladies became aware of the extent of the danger, when a young man fled across the road to avoid the speeding vehicle. But, instead of slowing up, Margrie used the whip once more. It was just after Louise screamed out in terror that the vehicle swerved and ran up a bank, causing it to topple onto its side. All the occupants were thrown into the road and the niece lost her shoes. But for her aunt it was much worse. She received severe injuries to her head and a fracture to one of the bones in her leg, which was protruding through the skin. Of course, there were no emergency services, so Louisa was taken immediately back to Dorchester in a cart, where she died seven days later, after having her leg

---

71   *Sherborne Mercury* 6/9/1845.
72   Part of the tack of a horse in harness which helps it to slow forward movement of a vehicle.

amputated. It had been established that Margrie had not been drunk, but several witnesses testified to the speed of the vehicle, and Dr William Tapp gave his view that the injuries sustained were the cause of death.

Although there were no official speed limits on the roads, the law on cases such as these was clear, as Justice Erle told the jury in his summing up. He told them that if they felt the accident occurred when the prisoner had no control of the horse, and that he had lost control by driving too fast, then he was guilty of manslaughter. He added that the public must not be given the message, through their verdict, that a person could drive at a furious pace on a turnpike road without liability if an accident happened. The judge then went over the evidence again and, according to the reporter of the *Chronicle*, he appeared to be of the opinion that Margrie had driven at an improper pace.[73]

The defence argued that his client had no case to answer for because there was no act of negligence involved. The crash was an accident, and there was no intent on the driver's part to cause injury. Why, he asked, would a man put his wife and children in jeopardy by driving so furiously? As a coda to his address and a final attempt to sway the jury, he mentioned that the accused had already spent seven months in prison awaiting trial.

It took but a few minutes for the jury to inform the judge of their not guilty verdict, but added that something should be brought against Margrie for furious driving. Erle reiterated the law and told them to think again. They did so and returned with the same verdict. Margrie walked from the court a free man.

***

The case of Crofts against Waterhouse was heard in the Nisi Prius court at the 1827 summer assizes. Mr Crofts was seeking compensation from the proprietor of the Swan with Two Necks for the actions taken by his servant, a coachman.

The Swan with Two Necks, which was situated in Lad Lane, Cripplegate, was one of London's main coaching inns. In 1829, 23 coaches each day were leaving there for Manchester and Liverpool in the north, Reigate and Southampton in the south, and Falmouth and Penzance in the west. Mr

---

73   *Chronicle* 19/3/1846.

The Swan with Two Necks, Lad Lane, Cripplegate, where Mr Crofts began his ill-fated journey. First mentioned in 1556, it was one of London's oldest and most well-known coaching inns. (Source, London Old and New, Vol 3, W. Thornbury, 1906.)

Crofts, who was a grocer, had business in the West Country and duly booked himself an outside seat on the stagecoach named *Regulator*, departing for Exeter. On the due date Mr Crofts took his seat on the coach, which had a full complement of passengers and, according to the *Chronicle*,[74] more luggage than should have been allowed. The coachman, a man named Beckley, was not in the best of humour when he climbed up onto his box. One witness told the court that he was in a sullen mood and had used profane language in an argument with another man at the inn.

The journey to Exeter would take them via Salisbury and after spending the night in that city the *Regulator* set off between 5 and 6 o'clock in the morning. It was a fine dawn, no lamps were necessary, and the journey had been uneventful, until they reached the bottom of Harnham Hill that is. Near the bottom of the hill there was a right-angle turn and according to the prosecution the coachman pulled his horses too far over to the other side of

---

74   *Chronicle* 28/7/1827.

the road as he negotiated it. This caused the wheels to go up an embankment and the coach overturned, throwing everyone on the outside into the road. Serjeant Pell, representing Crofts, told the court that the previous day a cottage had been taken down on that very spot and part of a footpath cut away to make room for the rubbish, and it was among this that the wheels were entangled. Mr Crofts was seriously injured, but as he had no friends nearby he had to continue his journey, this time inside the coach, until he reached Littlebredy Hut near Bridport where his sister lived. He remained there under the care of Dr Sweeting of Bridport, who stated that his patient was in extreme danger.

Several witnesses supported the assertions of Pell, all saying that the coach was on the wrong side of the road. Prima facie it was an open and shut case, but Serjeant Wilde put up a spirited defence, starting by telling the jury to be cautious about the evidence of the passengers, as the view they had was 'actuated by irritated feelings and whose ignorance of the subject should prevent any weight being given to their opinions on the subject of driving'.[75] On the point of the demeanour and language of the driver when they set off, he reminded them that coachmen were not bred at universities, and that they learned their language from those amongst whom they lived. As to the driver being on the wrong side of the road, he asserted that at 2 o'clock in the morning there was no right side of the road. In mitigation he introduced the evidence of the driver and the guard who both said that the disappearance of the cottage the day before was the sole reason for the accident because it was used by the driver to determine his line of approach to the corner, and that he had to pull over to the right to get back on track, causing the coach to collide with the rubbish.

In his summing up Justice Littledale said that even if the coachman had to drive onto the wrong side of the road, he had no business to be off the road. After about an hour of deliberation the jury found for the plaintiff and awarded damages of £100.

∗∗∗

---

75   Ibid.

A case presented to the court in 1866 was unusual in that it was brought by a 7-year-old child who was suing for injuries incurred by him because of a coach crash. The story began when his father, William Hardy, a London stockbroker, decided to take his family away from the capital for a holiday in Swanage, Dorset. It was decided that they would take the train to Wareham and then travel on to their seaside lodgings by omnibus, where they were to spend a month. The party consisted of Mr Hardy and his wife, their five children, two nieces and two nurses. All went well on the journey until the bus was about two miles from its destination, when the near-hind wheel gave way, and all the outside passengers were thrown to the ground. Several were badly bruised, but nobody was seriously hurt except the young lad Hardy, who had sustained a commuted fracture[76] of the leg. The father decided to stay in Swanage and the boy was wheeled around in a bath chair. It was twelve weeks before the family could go back to London and William Hardy incurred considerable expenses for medical care, lodgings for his family and train fares to and from London necessitated by his business. In respect of the child's injuries the father said that, although his son was likely to suffer long term from the effects of the crash, he was prepared to compromise on the costs, but only if the defendant accepted liability.

The defendant, Cornelius Yearsley, owner of the omnibus and keeper of the Red Lion, Wareham, decided not to accept the offer and went ahead with defending the case. He told the court that some of the spokes of the broken wheel had been recently replaced and in his opinion the wheel was sound. The driver of the bus, who had worked for Yearsley for five years and was considered a careful driver, gave his view on what had caused the accident. He said that it occurred on a steep hill, where the road had a high camber and was just 13 or 14 ft wide. In addition, there was a water channel on the side of the highway. Just as he was approaching a short curve in the road he saw a gig coming towards him at the trot and in order to avoid it he had to drive into the channel. It was when he tried to return to the road that the weight of the omnibus caused the wheel to fail. The judge told the jury that the driver was clearly not at fault and what they had to decide was whether the wheel was sound. After just a few minutes consultation they found for the defendant.

***

---

76   A fracture of the bone into more than two fragments.

A person wishing to travel from one end of the country to the other by coach could do so and to this end a network of routes existed, but, and like today, the efficiency of the system depended on timely connections, and also like today things did not always go to plan. The 70-year-old woman who arrived in Bradford-on-Avon in Wiltshire in June 1817, in a fly,[77] was not happy. Her journey had begun in London, at the offices of the proprietors of what was called the 'Companies Coach', who ran a passenger coach service to Bristol. The company operated in a different way to most because passengers did not have to pay separately for the guards and drivers, nor for the buglers or wind music that entertained travellers on their journey. The lady passenger had a slight problem. The London coach did not go through Bradford, so to get there she had to transfer to another coach from Melksham. The Bristol coach duly arrived in Melksham and then proceeded on its journey. It was a few miles outside the city of Bath that the woman woke up and realised she had missed her stop by some miles.

She spoke to the guard, who was less than sympathetic. He suggested that she get off the coach and walk cross country to Bradford with her two large boxes, adding that the weather was fine, and the walk would do her good. Declining his offer, the woman stayed on the coach until it reached Bath where she had to hire the fly to take her to Bradford, at a cost of ten shillings.

The offended lady decided to recover the cost of having to hire the carriage at the Dorchester assizes, but for some reason the action was not brought by her but by a Mr Flight. In their defence the coach company said that for half a mile before they had arrived at the place where the branch coach was waiting, the guard had not ceased to blow and play upon his bugle, and that upon arriving at the spot he opened the door and enquired if any of the passengers were going to Bradford; a voice from within said 'No'. They also claimed that the coach remained there for twenty minutes before moving on. The jury was not impressed by this defence and awarded the plaintiff damages of ten shillings. This case generated considerable interest and lasted all day because it involved an important point of contract. Given the coach company knew that the lady wanted to join the feeder coach at Melksham, to what degree was the guard obliged to make sure that she got off. On a lighter side, the newspaper *Bell's Weekly Messenger*[78] could not help itself by headlining its article on the case 'Going a stage too far'.[79]

---

77 A lightweight carriage.
78 *Bell's Weekly Messenger* was published between 1796 and 1896.
79 *Bell's Weekly Messenger* 23/3/1818.

A Woman Scorned

In July 1856, a petition was raised in the Dorset town of Poole, addressed 'To the Queen's most Excellent Majesty'. It read:

'The humble petition of the undersigned Inhabitants of the Town and County of Poole, humbly showeth – That at the last assize for the County of Dorset, held at Dorchester, Elizabeth Martha Brown, was indicted for the wilful murder of her husband, John Anthony Brown, convicted and sentenced to be hung; and now awaits at Dorchester Gaol the execution of the sentence. That your petitioners are firmly and solemnly convinced that neither the matter of evidence produced at the trial nor subsequent enquiry has shown that the act, which resulted in the death of the deceased was indicated; but that such evidence and enquiries fully satisfy your Petitioners that the blows inflicted were given in a paroxysm of anger, produced on the instant by the state in which the unfortunate deceased arrived at his dwelling, and the treatment then and there experienced at his hand; and they are confirmed in this conviction by the results of information obtained of the previous character of the unfortunate woman, which, they learn, has been uniformly, humane and moral. Your Petitioners would further draw attention to the difficulty, acknowledged by the prosecution of discovering a motive for the act, the first being, as your Petitioners firmly believe, that the momentary anger in her breast was the first and only propellant of the deed. Your Petitioners therefore pray your Majesty's benign consideration of the above circumstances.'[80]

This was just one of several petitions that were raised around Dorset whilst Elizabeth Martha Brown, known as Martha, was sitting in Dorchester gaol awaiting the death sentence. Had their pleas been based just on the evidence that came out at her trial they may not have put pen to paper, because it was compellingly against her plea of not guilty.

Martha told the police investigating her husband John's death that on Saturday 5 July [81] 1856 he left their home in the hamlet of Birdsmoorgate to deliver some wooden poles to Beaminster, a town about seven miles away. She saw nothing more of him until 2 o'clock the next morning, when she heard someone groaning under the window of her cottage, and when she investigated she found him on the floor in a terrible state, bleeding from wounds in the head. She heard him say in a barely audible voice, 'The horse'. Martha said that with great difficulty she managed to drag him into the

---

80   *Poole and South Western Herald* 31/7/1856.
81   John's grave gives his death as 6 July.

cottage but was then unable to go for help until four hours later because he held a grip on her dress from which she could not escape. Eventually she managed to do so and went to the house of a relative about a hundred yards away to get help. It was when she returned to the room where he lay that she heard her husband give a few short breaths and die. She was sure the horse, which could be unpredictable, had kicked him.

At the inquest into John's death the initial verdict was one of wilful murder by person or persons unknown, but after appearing before the magistrates Martha was committed to Dorchester gaol to await her trial for murdering him. A Mr Stock was counsel for the prosecution and after detailing the facts of the case he presented a string of witnesses whose evidence would gradually destroy the credulity of Martha's version of events. Thomas Fooks, who was a fellow carrier, went to Beaminster with John Brown, and he saw John's body soon after the death. He told the court that there was no blood in the doorway of the cottage, which would have been expected if the wife had dragged the profusely bleeding body of her husband inside. He also stated that on their way back to Birdsmoorgate he and Brown had stopped off and had a considerable amount to drink, but he did not think that his friend was visibly drunk.

John Brown's grave, in Holy Trinity churchyard, Blackdown, near Beaminster. The inscription reads: 'To the Memory of John A Brown whose life was taken away July 6th 1856 in the 26th year of his Age. Amiable and affectionate in his Disposition, Kind and Generous in his Conduct, He was sincerely Beloved and will long be lamented by his kindred and Friends.' (Author copyright.)

Widow Harriet Knight lived near to the Browns. She contested that she heard the field gate where Brown's horse was kept shut at about 2 am, and also heard footsteps. She could not be sure but she thought she recognised them as John's. She could then hear the horse eating grass. At 5 am she was woken from her slumber by Richard Damon who begged her to get up and go to the Brown's house. Martha told her what had happened, but Harriet could not help but ask how she could sit there so long without getting help for her husband. Harriet noted that blood was flowing freely from John's head onto the floor and when she removed a handkerchief that was covering it Martha told her to put it down and tell no one.

Next to give evidence was Hanna Smith, who noted that there was no dirt on John's trousers or coat, as if he had been crawling outside. She then had the curiosity to examine the road from the field, where she found no trace of blood. It was John Damon who went down to the field to see if there was any evidence of what had happened. There he found on a gatepost John's hat, which had no signs of being damaged, but he could not think that it could have got there by being kicked through the gate by the horse. On cross-examination Damon attested that the Browns had a hatchet which had now gone missing. Another witness, Elizabeth Sampson, appeared to be the only person who actually heard what allegedly had happened. She swore that there were three loud shrieks and groans which appeared to come from the Browns' house, which unsettled her so much that she was unable to get back to sleep.

Respectability was added to the prosecution's list of witnesses when Mr De La Fosse, curate of Broadwindsor, was called to the stand. He contended that he visited Martha a few days after the event and she told him, 'I am accused of murdering my husband, but am as innocent as the angels in heaven'.[82] He was quick to tell her that he had accused her of nothing, but that the absence of blood everywhere except in the room they were sitting seemed to show that he had not been kicked by a horse, but had been injured in the room. She then asked, 'What should make me kill him, to lose my home, and have to lie out under a hedge?'[83] Others were present at the time De La Fosse visited and he could not help noticing that among the people present in the room Martha was the only one who appeared to be unmoved. John's mother who was there fainted and others were in tears. Despite her apparent apathy she did have a point: what was the motive?

When they married, John was just 19 and Martha was in her late 30s. She was an attractive woman, some said beautiful, and she had some wealth, gained from the shop she ran in the village. The marriage produced one child, but, on the whole it was not a happy one. John's work took him away from home and he often returned home the worse for drink. The other element in the marriage was Mary Davis, a younger woman whose exact relationship with the couple is unclear. Certainly there was gossip among the local villages that there was something going on between her and John, and on the day John went to deliver the poles the young woman jumped up

---

82   *Chronicle* 24/7/1856.
83   Ibid.

on his cart and shared some of the journey before getting off again to go and work in the fields. If Martha did murder her husband perhaps the motive was jealousy. One witness, Susan Damon, who was in tears when she came to give evidence, said that Martha had referred to Mary Davis as 'an old wench' or 'an old bitch, or something like that'. Jim Lane, who was a young man at the time, had no doubts about John and Mary Davis's relationship. Speaking to Lady Hester Pinney in the 1920s he told her:

> 'John Brown he did bide about with her [Mary Davis] – a bad man. Martha went along there one night and found her husband on Mary Powell's[84] knee. ... Mary had money and I suppose John liked the younger woman better, she was younger and smarter, but Martha was a nice looking lady too.'[85]

The medical evidence was damning. Dr Richard Brosier, who had conducted the post-mortem with Dr Joachim Gilbert, after describing the considerable number of wounds to the head, was of the opinion that, given the extent and nature of them, if they had been inflicted in the field there would have been traces of blood on the road and down the front of John's shirt. Also, in his opinion, the dead man would have been paralysed after about the third blow and would not have been able to crawl up to his home, and neither would he have been able to talk. In short, he felt, as did his colleague, that death would have occurred immediately after the blows were inflicted.

Mr Edwards, the defence lawyer, chose not to summon Martha to the witness box, concerned perhaps at how she might perform under cross-examination. Instead, he was going to rely on his powers of persuasion. He opened by accusing the prosecution of persecution. Under the law Martha should have had every means afforded her for her defence. He claimed that this had not been the case, because much of the prosecution's evidence had been withheld from her. Several witnesses had not appeared at the magistrate's hearing and the first she heard of what they had to say was at this trial. Nothing, for example, had been said until that day about the Browns owning a hatchet that could not be found. Had Mrs Brown known that it was significant, then doubtless she would have produced it.

Edwards then asserted that all the evidence was circumstantial and that everything that had been said by the witnesses only confirmed the innocence

---

84 Mary Davis married for a second time and became Mary Powell.
85 Contained in a letter from Lady Hester Pinney to Thomas Hardy regarding the case of Martha Brown, dated 16/1/1926.

of the accused. He also pointed to the view of Dr Gilbert that the blows that caused the injuries must have been carried out with considerable force, surely something the prisoner did not have the strength to do. Neither could they place any confidence in what had been stated about the relationship between John and Mary Davis, and clearly Martha was not a jealous woman. The very night he did not come home she had prepared a supper for him, not the act of a woman with murder in her mind. In fact, there was no reason to suspect that they were anything but a happy couple.

The giving of evidence and submissions had now concluded, and it was time for the judge, Serjeant Channell, to address the jury. He reminded them of the gravity of their position and said that it was upon the evidence that they should convict, and should there be any doubt it was their duty to acquit. The first question for them to address was whether the wounds were inflicted in the room and, secondly, if they were, who had inflicted them. The jury left the courtroom at 6.10 pm and it was not until about 10 pm that the judge felt obliged to call them back. They had not reached a verdict. They wanted to ask the surgeon if the skull bones could have been driven further into the brain by moving the body and, also, if the deceased could have got back into the house with the aid of his wife. In answer to both he said no. The twelve men then conferred for a few minutes and declared their verdict of guilty. After putting on the black cap the judge implored the condemned woman to endeavour to obtain pardon and forgiveness from the God whom she had so awfully and wickedly offended. When sentence was being passed Martha seemed quite unmoved, but as she was taken back down into the cells she kept muttering that she was innocent.

The date of the hanging was set for 9 August, allowing time for her to make her peace with God and make her confession. After several attempts to persuade her to confess she finally dictated a statement to the prison governor, just two days before her execution. In it she said:

'My husband John Anthony Brown, deceased, came home on Sunday morning, the 6th of July at 2 o'clock, in liquor, and was sick. He had no hat on. I asked him what he had done with his hat. He abused me, and said: "What is it to you, _____ you?"[86] He then asked for some cold tea. I said that I had none, but I would make some warm. He replied, "Drink it yourself, and be _____". I then said, "What makes you so cross? Have you been at Mary Davis's?" He then kicked out the bottom of the chair upon which I had been sitting. We continued quarrelling until 3 o'clock, when he struck me a severe blow on the side of my head, which

---

86   Expletive omitted in newspaper report.

confused me so much that I was obliged to sit down. Supper was on the table, and he said, "Eat it yourself, and be ____". At the same time, he reached down from the mantelpiece a heavy horsewhip with a plaid end and struck me across the shoulders with it three times. Each time I screamed out. I said, "If you strike me again I will cry murder". He retorted, "If you do, I will knock your brains out through the window". He also added, "I hope I shall find you dead in the morning". He then kicked me on the left side, which caused much pain, and he immediately stooped down to untie his boots. I was much enraged, and in an ungovernable passion, on being so abused and struck, I directly seized a hatchet which was lying close to where I sat, and which I had been using to break coal with to keep up the fire and keep the supper warm, and with it I struck him several violent blows on the head, I could not say how many. He fell at the first blow on his head, with his face toward the fireplace. He never spoke or moved afterwards. As soon as I had done it I wished I had not, and would have given the world not to have done it. I had never struck him before, after all his ill-treatment; but when he hit me so hard at this time, I was almost out of my senses and hardly knew what I was doing.'[87]

Had Martha made her confession earlier the outcome of her life may have been different. It may well have been sufficient to gain a reprieve. All the petitions raised had been refused, but there was just time for another attempt to save her life. The prison chaplain dashed up to London in the hope of seeing the Home Secretary Sir George Grey, but unfortunately he was out of the country and his deputy did not have the power to make a decision.

Martha's execution, the last woman to be hanged publically in Dorchester, had none of the morbid raucous behaviour of the audience usually associated with public hangings. Reporters of the *Southern Times* were present and described the event graphically, even poetically:

'We arrived at the scaffold at half-past seven, and upon reaching the fatal platform we found the grim apparatus of death ready for its fearful mission; a sultry heat pervaded the atmosphere, and rain fell fast and thick upon the upturned faces of about 2,000 spectators. There was no shouting, no ribald jesting, no obscene levity, no noise or uproar in the crowd; a dull melancholy appeared to have taken possession of the popular mind, and the people evidently sympathised with the victim, who in a few minutes was to be plunged o'er the precipice of time into the gulf of eternity before their eyes. Executioner Calcraft, who had slept in the gaol the night before, ascended the steps to ascertain that the engine of death was complete in all its appointments, and having critically examined the drop, the lever, and bolt, he quickly retired; as we turned our backs upon the crowd we saw

---

87   *Cheshire Observer and General Advertiser* 18/8/1856.

two men approaching down the broad walk of the prison grounds carrying on their shoulders a coffin, the living tenant of which was at that moment receiving, at the hands of the Chaplain, the sacrament, and the last consolations of his holy office. As the clock struck eight the heavy tolling of the death knell prepared the masses for the final act of drama, and at the same time the Under-Sheriff and his attendants, with their wands and staves, the Governor of the gaol, the wretched criminal, supported by a female warder, the Chaplain and another Clergyman, and the Executioner, moved in solemn order towards the drop. Upon every countenance in that mournful group sorrow sat in unmistakable guise; many were moved to tears – whilst the feelings of the worthy kind-hearted Chaplain so far overcame him that he was unable to proceed beyond the first step of the scaffold. At the top of the steps the "death toilet" took place. Calcraft requested the convict to remove her bonnet, with which she immediately complied; he then pinioned her arms with a black leather strap, and having turned down the collar of her dress, the procession went up the second series of steps that led to the gallows. Arriving upon that fatal plank, the indistinct hum of the crowd was hushed; not a whisper was audible. Calcraft placed her under the beam, pulled the cap over her eyes, secured the rope, shook her trembling hands, and hastened to the bolt; for a few seconds this wretched form of humanity was gently rocked by the agony of her mind; one convulsive heave of the bosom was perceptible, the trap fell, and Martha Brown died without a struggle. The body of that ill-fated woman swayed in the morning air a victim to a mischievous and demoralising law.' [88]

The former entrance to the county gaol, in North Square, over which Martha Brown was hanged. (Courtesy of Dorset Museum.)

88 *Southern Times* 16/8/1856.

The article in which the above appears also contains a condemnation of the verdict, seeing her crime as an act of passion, requiring a charge of manslaughter and not premeditated murder. In fact, even before the execution, the case of Martha Brown ignited considerable debate in newspapers about the validity of capital punishment in society and the treatment of women by the judicial system.

Martha Brown has become part of Dorset folklore, not just because of the controversy surrounding the verdict, but also because in the crowd that day was a 16-year-old boy named Thomas Hardy, who would go on to become an author. He wrote very prosaically about what he saw. The event obviously haunted him because when he was in his 80s he admitted that he was ashamed at being there and that his only excuse was that he was a youth and happened to be in Dorchester on the day for something else. It is supposed that the author based his character Tess, in his book *Tess of the D'Urbervilles*, on Martha.

Affairs of the Heart

At the summer assizes of 1818 Serjeant Pell stood up and told the Special Jury that, 'If his instructions were correct, and the allegations on which the charge was founded was found to be substantiated, then he should be justified in saying that it was an instance of almost unprecedented combination of treachery, guilt and cruelty, formed for the overthrow of innocence and happiness'.[89] He added that, 'should the story they were about to hear turn out to be false his client', a 16-year-old girl, 'could be nothing less than a monster of treachery, and had arrived at a climax of infamy unexampled in the annals of human guilt'.[90] The girl he was referring to, Maria Glenn, was the alleged victim of the crime of abduction in the case of The King v Bowditch and others. Those accused of being involved in conspiring to have taken and carried away Maria and to procure a marriage between her and James Bowditch were James Bowditch, William Bowditch, Joan Bowditch, Susanna Bowditch, Elizabeth Gibbons, Susanna Mulraine, Jane Marks, Thomas Paul and Elizabeth Snell. The main defendants were the Bowditches, Susannah Mulraine and Thomas Paul, but the others were accused of being complicit in the crime. This criminal case was brought by the girl's uncle and the verdict was to have repercussions beyond the county of Dorset.

At about the age of nine, Maria Glenn arrived in England, after a long boat journey from the West Indies. Back in St Vincent her widowed mother Mary Glenn had decided to send her daughter to England to complete her education. Mary's husband, William Glenn, had been a barrister, who had died when Maria was 3 years old and, since his death, mother, daughter and grandmother had lived together on a small income. Whilst Maria's immediate financial circumstances were modest, her prospects for the future were better. Her grandfather owned two large sugar plantations which, eventually, she should inherit, making her a very desirable catch for any prospective husband. In looks Maria was described as a plain child, a characteristic that was reflected in her dress. Her dresses were plain white muslin, worn with a shawl or, in winter, a pelisse,[91] and she always wore a broad brimmed bonnet when she was out.

---

89   *London Times* 28/7/1818.
90   Ibid.
91   A long, high-waisted, loose coat.

In character the young lady was shy and retiring and must have felt considerable apprehension in leaving her close-knit family and going into the unknown. Fortunately, waiting for Maria in England was her uncle and guardian George Tuckett, who lived in Taunton with his wife Martha and their five children.

George Lowman Tuckett was born in 1771 in Bridgewater and was educated in Exeter and then at St John's College, Cambridge where he studied law and eventually followed his father into that profession. Even as a young man he was principled and believed in doing the right thing, and as an adult he was sober, rational and industrious. Ironically, he was a close acquaintance of the poet Samuel Taylor Coleridge[92] who in character was just the opposite. Living in Taunton with George was his wife Martha and five children. Maria fitted in well with the Tucketts. Her loving nature soon drew the children toward her, especially the youngest ones, Lucretia and Gertrude, who treated her like a sister. For her education Maria first went to a boarding school in Exeter, but she was very unhappy there. She got on well with the teachers but not with the other pupils, who did not like her and did not play with her. After putting

Maria wore a pelisse, like the one shown here, and always wore a wide brimmed bonnet. (Courtesy of LAMCA.)

up with three years of unhappiness she persuaded her guardians to move her to another school, but she was just as unhappy there. Finally, they sent her to a day school attended by her cousins. As well as having Maria to help them look after the younger children, the Tucketts employed a nursemaid,

92   Samuel Taylor Coleridge (1772–1834), co-founder of the Romantic movement of poetry with William Wordsworth, and one of the Lakeland poets.

13-year-old Mary Ann Whitby, a friendly and literate girl from a poor family of nonconformists, who was to play a leading role in Maria's story.

A few months after Mary Ann arrived, disaster struck the family, when Maria and two of the Tuckett girls became ill. At first it was assumed that they all had colds, but their symptoms got worse and finally whooping cough was diagnosed, a killer at that time. Luckily, through careful nursing, they all survived but Maria was left with a terrible cough. Concerned about this, George asked a doctor friend for advice. His recommendation was to send all the girls away to recuperate in the countryside. A former schoolmistress of Maria's suggested that they should go to Holway Green Farm, a place where she had once lodged and within walking distance of the Tuckett house. Widow Joan Bowditch farmed the land with the help of some of her older children and there was plenty of room in the house for paying guests. Maria, her young cousins and Mary Ann would share a bedroom and live separately from the Bowditches. Their food would be delivered to them each day by Mary Ann, who would help with the children.

Joan Bowditch had a large family – six daughters and two sons, some of whom were still living at home and worked on the farm; Susanna, Sarah and Betsy were employed in the dairy and helped to look after the house, whilst the youngest son James, aged 25, worked as a labourer in the fields. Of those who were not at home, one daughter was married to James Scarlett, a printer and journalist at the *Taunton Courier*, and another was married to Thomas Paul, a gentleman who lived in a grand house in Thornford, Dorset. Twenty-one-year-old Ann worked in Ireland as a servant and the second son, William, was an innkeeper in Taunton.

When Maria and her cousins joined the Bowditch household they found it very different to their own. In contrast to the genteel lifestyle at home they found that the family were extravert, loud and liked to play boisterous games like blind man's bluff. One woman, who Maria liked particularly, was Mrs Mulraine, a friend of Mrs Bowditch, who visited Holway Green often. She was an educated woman who promised Maria that she would teach her how to paint and draw on velvet. Maria's relationship with the Bowditch family was affable. She was invited to ride Jane's pony and on a couple of occasions James Bowditch accompanied her and her cousins when they walked to visit her uncle and aunt, the latter not thinking it appropriate for the girls to do so unaccompanied.

The girls' health improved in the countryside, to the extent that after four months George and Martha Tuckett decided that it was time for them to return home. One day, just before the girls were due to leave, George visited

Holway Green Farm and found it unusually quiet. Enquiring of Maria why that was, she explained that the family were attending the christening of Mrs Mulraine's little girl in Taunton. In fact, they had asked Maria to be a godmother to the child, but she declined. The christening was to play a pivotal role in the future court case.

It was agreed that the girls would return home on 2 September and Mr and Mrs Tuckett went to Holway to deliver the news. After they left, Jane and Mrs Mulraine went to Maria's room and asked if she really intended leaving. She said that she was, to which Joan Bowditch exclaimed that her son was bereft and she did not know what to do with him. Maria asked her what she meant. At this point Mrs Mulraine interjected, saying, 'Surely you could not be ignorant, nor been in the house so long not to notice that James Bowditch has an attachment to you?'[93] Maria was astonished, asking them what they thought her uncle and aunt would think about such a thing, and told them to talk no more of it as it distressed her. The two women left her, but the next day Mrs Mulraine entreated her to speak to James, who she said was distracted at her leaving and the family could not reason with him. Perhaps if she spoke to him he would be realistic about their different conditions in society that made a relationship impossible. At this point Maria needed to escape the conversation, so she left the room and went to her bedroom. Nothing more was said on the matter for a couple of days, but the day before Maria was due to leave Mrs Mulraine went to her in the parlour and beseeched her to speak to James, whom she claimed was threatening suicide. Maria refused.

The next day Maria returned home, but if she thought that was an end to the matter she was wrong. About a week later Joan Bowditch turned up at the house, accompanied by Mrs Mulraine and another woman. They asked if they could go for a walk with Maria, but her aunt, who was upstairs at the time, said no. Instead the four of them sat in the parlour where the former conversation regarding James Bowditch was reintroduced. During the discourse Joan Bowditch said something that must have put fear into Maria's heart. She was told that James had declared that he would not live without her, but would rather murder both her and himself. Mrs Mulraine added that he proclaimed that he was prepared to follow Maria to any part of the world and would destroy her, and added that if she told her uncle and aunt the danger would only be greater. To complete the threat Maria was advised to reflect on what a shocking thing it would be to be murdered, and to swear on her life that she would do what James wanted. Under such intimidation

---

93   *Westmorland Gazette and Kendal Advertiser* 18/8/1818.

the teenager said 'Yes', and with the threat of murder over her head she dared not tell her uncle or aunt.

In the witness box, Maria told the court what happened next. On Saturday 20 September as she was walking alone in Taunton she was met by James Bowditch and Mrs Mulraine. The latter told her to go with them because she wanted to tell her something. Of course, Maria refused, causing James to cry out with a fierce look on his face, 'Go! Go! You know what I have declared. I'll do it!' Under such a threat Maria went with them to a house in East Street, where she was presented with a piece of paper which they cajoled her into signing. Then a man entered the room whom she later recognised to be a Mr Oxenham, a Taunton solicitor. He put another paper in front of her, which she thought had Greek lettering, and told her to sign it, which she did with a trembling hand, Bowditch and Mulraine standing on each side of her. Now, she was told, she would no longer be molested.

Just before Maria's return home the Tucketts had made a decision that would have dire consequences for their niece. They had decided that she should continue her education and arranged for her to attend a boarding school in London. Of course, the Bowditch party knew nothing of this. That was until the day after Maria was forced to sign the paper. She and her aunt were returning from church when she was told the news, that in a day or two's time she was going to a boarding school in Chelsea. Significantly, Joan Bowditch happened to be walking alongside them and overheard what was said.

Surprisingly, considering her previous unhappy days of schooling, Maria seemed well disposed to the idea, doubtless relieved to be able to get away from the danger in Taunton. That night she went to bed between 9 and 10 o'clock in a room next to her uncle's bedroom, which she shared with her cousins. Maria said that she soon fell asleep, and the next thing she recollected was being woken by Jane Marks the Tucketts' cook, who said, 'Get up, they are waiting for you, and you know what Mr Bowditch has said'.[94] Jane then got the confused and frightened girl out of bed and dressed her. Maria declared that she was too frightened to cry out. Next, she was pulled downstairs and taken out of the house through her uncle's study window, which the day before James' brother William had told one of the Tucketts' maids to leave open. Waiting outside were James Bowditch, William and others, who took her to Holway Green Farm. There she was led to the kitchen and forced to drink a cup of something black and bitter like medicine. After being given

---

94   Ibid.

another dose the young girl was taken to the house of Joan Bowditch's son-in-law Thomas Paul, at Thornford near Sherborne. Maria said she remembered nothing of the journey. Mr Paul was reportedly exulted at Maria's arrival and exclaimed, 'We shall now have all the bells in the village ringing'.[95] They then took her to a room where a tall man was sitting in the corner, reading some papers. It was claimed that he was Richard Gould, a labourer from an adjoining village, who was pretending to be a clergyman. He asked Maria how old she was and when she said sixteen he declared that the marriage would be illegal, but when Bowditch gave him a severe look he added, 'Never mind you may be married just as well'.[96] After dinner, which she attended against her will, Maria went upstairs and endeavoured to write a letter, but she was interrupted by James who snatched it from her, and said that nobody could blame him if he used her unkindly, and called her a little b_____h [sic].

It was Martha Tuckett who first became aware that Maria was missing. She was feeling unwell when she retired and went to Maria's room to elicit some help. She found that not only was her bed empty, but she was nowhere to be found in the house. Her husband's first act, after searching the house himself and finding the open window, was to interrogate the servants. They told him that they knew nothing, but he thought he heard one of them whisper to another the word 'Bowditch'. After questioning, Mary Ann told him that she believed his niece might have eloped with James Bowditch.

That evening George Tuckett rushed to his solicitor's office, fearing that his niece might already be on her way to Gretna Green. On the way he met Mrs Mulraine who asked him if he had any news, and, clearly wishing to distance herself from the whole affair, told him that Maria had been taken to Mr Paul's house at Thornford, and that she had had nothing to do with the affair. Within an hour George's solicitor, Henry Leigh, was in a chaise and four on his way to Thornford, with two of Taunton's bailiffs. Luckily, the next morning the Bowditch men were out shooting when Leigh approached Paul's house. He entered and standing before him was Maria, whom he told must go with him. Asked why, he said that he was going to take her home. Safely back at home Maria told her uncle and aunt that far from eloping she had been forced, although James Bowditch had not touched her. Nevertheless, George sent for a doctor.

When Mr Robert Casberd took the floor of the court to open for the defence he recognised that if he could not overthrow the evidence of Maria

---

95   Ibid.
96   Ibid.

Glenn then his case was hopeless. In his attempt to do so he produced no less than sixteen witnesses, most of whom were related to the Bowditch family or were in some way dependent upon them. Many said that they had seen the couple walking arm in arm. A Mrs Warren said she lived opposite the Tucketts and on one occasion saw Maria chasing after James into French Wear Field, where, after looking back at her uncle's house, she took his arm and walked on. On cross-examination she could not remember the day, although she thought it very inappropriate behaviour. Another witness, James Bowditch's sister Sarah claimed, 'I observed a great deal of impropriety in Miss Glenn's behaviour with regard to my brother, such as treading upon his toes, and throwing her handkerchief at him'.[97]

The Bowditches had always contended that Maria was present at the christening of Mrs Mulraine's child, something she denied emphatically. However, Mary Priest, who lived in Taunton, claimed not only that Maria was present but also that she and James Bowditch were the godparents.

Joseph Brown, a labourer employed by Joan Bowditch, testified that one day whilst he was working in a field Miss Glenn and James Bowditch stopped and Maria told him that she was going to be married to Mr Bowditch, and before the couple went off towards St Mary Magdalen's church she showed him a wedding ring and said she was going to be married with it. About two hours later when they returned and Brown asked 'Miss, is the knot tied?' she answered, 'Yes, thank God, and it cannot be untied'.[98]

If the testimony of these witnesses and others was true then Maria Glenn's version of what had happened would prove to be a pack of lies. However, the words of one of the attesters did not help the defence. Samuel Mansfield contended that he had seen James and Maria walking together many times arm in arm. He even saw them on one occasion kissing in a wagon and on another she was sitting on his knee in the kitchen. At this point counsel for the prosecution brought Maria back into the courtroom from the lobby, where she had been sitting with Mary Ann Whitby. Serjeant Pell told Mansfield to turn round and look at her and then asked him if this was the girl he had seen sitting on James' knee. He replied, 'No, this is not the young lady'. This caused astonishment in the court and 'a strong feeling of indignation was manifested',[99] suggesting that there was no shortage of Bowditch supporters on the public benches. When asked if the lady present was the one he saw kissing on the hay wagon, the witness again replied in the negative, which

---

97   Ibid.
98   Ibid.
99   Ibid.

brought forth even more indignation from those in the court, to the extent that it was some minutes before order was restored.

It had been a long and tiring day when Serjeant Pell rose in the court to answer a question from the judge. He was interrupted by Henry Bankes,[100] foreman of the jury, who asked for a few minutes for the jury to consult, and after they had he declared that they had come to a conclusion and there was no need for the judge to sum up. The jury decided that all the accused, except Elizabeth Snell, the housemaid, were guilty of a conspiracy. Justice Park concurred with the jury and went further, saying that the defence was full of infamy and complimented Maria on her patient resignation to the gross and abominable aspersions which the defendants were continuously throwing at her.

The Bowditch family were down but not out. Far from accepting the verdict they decided to apply to the Court of King's Bench in London for a retrial. This would not be heard by a Special Jury chosen by the prosecution and consisting of men more akin perhaps to Maria's class than James's, but by a panel of judges. Despite the submission of between eighty and a hundred petitions, and the repeat of much of the evidence indicating that there was a relationship between the couple, a retrial was denied and sentences were handed out. Joan Bowditch and her son were sentenced to twenty-one months imprisonment, Mrs Mulraine to two years and James Bowditch to eighteen months.

The Bowditches had enjoyed much support from a large section of the population of Taunton and it seems that as the fight progressed the hostility towards Maria and the Tucketts increased, to the extent that one thousand copies of a notice were printed, to be posted around the town, accusing them of corrupt perjury, treachery, villainy and cruelty perpetrated on those incarcerated.

The convicted had been in prison about a month when George Tuckett received a letter from the uncle of Mary Ann Whitby, saying the Bowditches were contriving a plan to ensnare his niece and Maria. They were successful. On 20 September 1819, the two women found themselves in the Old Bailey facing the serious charge of perjury. Conviction would lead to shame and disgrace and potentially a heavy sentence in prison or transportation. Those that brought the charge were unknown, as there was no legal requirement to name those who had initiated the case, but Tuckett had a good idea of who was responsible. In the Old Bailey case, two points Mary Ann had mentioned

---

100   Henry Bankes (1757–1834), Dorset landowner and owner of Kingston Lacy house and estate, Wimborne.

in an affidavit pertinent to the original trial were picked out as being lies.

After the witnesses had come and gone and Lord Chief Justice had summed up, the jury found the two accused guilty. Mary Ann took the news calmly, but Maria became hysterical and had to be led away.

Next day, news of the verdict in London reached Taunton and immediately the church bells were rung, reportedly for three days, and festivities were arranged. When William Woodsford, a Taunton resident who had tried to help Maria Glenn, arrived home he had the coach stop outside the town and walked to his house through the back streets, hoping he would not meet anybody. Alongside the celebrations there was criticism of the original verdict. *The Examiner*, which had supported the Bowditches, referred to Justice Park as perhaps not the most temperate and discriminating judge.

On 27 November Mary Ann was ordered to appear at the Court of King's Bench in London for sentencing, but she did not turn up. She and Maria had fled. It was assumed that George Tuckett had smuggled the two girls away to the West Indies, but their whereabouts was nearer to home. George had hired a boat at Dover which took them to Boulogne in France, where eventually Maria settled, to be joined later by her mother and grandmother.

Mary Ann, under some pressure from her uncle, decided to return home and risk arrest. But before she went she told Maria, 'I assure you that whatever I might have to go through nothing shall ever make me say anything but what could prove your innocence or make me forget what I owe you for your goodness to me'.[101] Mary Ann was arrested in Bristol, but even before her trial at the Court of King's Bench on 13 May 1822 she had already compromised Maria by signing an affidavit stating that she and her mistress had lied previously. At the trial Mary Ann was reported to be 'Almost overwhelmed with affliction', but the court took pity on her and she was released on her own recognisances, agreeing to come before the court for judgement if required.

Maria Glenn remained in France and married twice. Her first husband was a soldier, Col de Salle, with whom she had two sons, and after his early death she married Sub Lt Etienne Dougnac of the Voltigeurs.[102] She had a daughter with him but the marriage was a calamity and they soon parted. Somehow Maria managed to smuggle herself back into England without her identity being discovered and after living in Kennington, South East London with her youngest son and her daughter she moved to Kent. She died of a heart

---

101   See Clifford.
102   Voltigeurs were skirmishers who vaulted onto their horses.

attack on 11 November 1866 and was buried in Canterbury. She never inherited her grandfather's fortune.

Mary Ann Whitby sank into obscurity after her trial, although a woman of that name did marry George Gunningham, in Charlton Mackrell, Somerset. As for the Bowditch family, despite the crippling legal fees they had to pay for the various court actions, Joan Bowditch continued farming at Holway Green and died in 1831, aged seventy-six. James Bowditch, the unsuccessful suitor, never married.

Maria in the 1860s. (Copyright Mark and Ann Hudson.)

***

William Stickland was a man who believed in long engagements. He was born in 1816 to a prosperous family who farmed Axnoller Farm, just outside Beaminster, and when he was twenty-four he took a fancy to a local beauty, Wilhelmina Milverton, daughter of a brewer who kept the Swan Inn[103] in Beaminster. The young man began to visit the inn on a regular basis and the couple often went into the private rooms, sometimes chaperoned by Wilhelmina's mother Ann, who felt that his attentions were those a lover might pay. Stickland's wooing became more ardent and time and time again he made it known that he would make her his wife, becoming very possessive of her. He would say to any man who paid her any attention, 'Keep off, she belongs to me, and is to be my wife'.[104] John Marsh, a local hairdresser, was a witness in the later trial and told of an occasion when a man named

---

103   The Swan Inn no longer exists. The building is now used as a library.
104   *Chronicle* 25/7/1861.

Bowditch[105] attempted to kiss Wilhelmina. He was quickly warned off by Stickland telling him, 'Leave her alone, or I will knock you down, I am going to marry her'. Marsh added that he had seen nobody kiss Wilhelmina, and he certainly would not do so himself after seeing what happened to Bowditch, which brought considerable laughter from the court.

In 1847 Wilhelmina's hopes of marriage must have risen when she gave birth to a baby boy. William did not contest the paternity of the child, although when it was christened his name was absent from the register. However, the mother attached a badge of ownership on the baby boy by naming him William Stickland Milverton. According to Wilhelmina's mother, she asked Stickland after the birth if he would now marry her daughter. He said, as he had on so many occasions, that he would do so when he had dissolved the business partnership with his brother. She added that he did occasionally pay money for the upkeep of the boy.

As the years went by there was still no sign of a proposal from the suiter, but he did at least put his intentions in writing, when in October 1859 he wrote a letter, stating that 'I William Stickland, of Axnoller Farm, do solemnly declare that I will marry Wilhelmina Milverton as soon as the lease of Axnoller Farm is expired. I will marry Wilhelmina Milverton and make her happy.'[106]

Despite this solemn declaration there were no nuptials on the horizon and the situation may have remained unchanged had not a dramatic twist occurred in the tale. On 16 May 1861, William Stickland married Sarah Paul, a lady of wealth, in Bath.

Wilhelmina had got wind of the marriage beforehand and instructed her solicitor to write a letter to him, asking when he was going to fulfil his promise. In reply, he denied that on any occasion did he ever volunteer to marry her, either verbally or in writing. Wilhelmina's reaction was to seek recompense in law, which she did at the summer assizes in 1861, in front of a special jury.[107]

At the time of the trial the Milverton family were struggling financially and were receiving relief from the parish, the equivalent of the dole today. The defence lawyer picked this up at the trial and said that this showed that the parents were not as respectable as the opposition had suggested.

---

105   The Bowditch in this case has no direct connection to the family mentioned in the case of Maria Glenn.
106   Ibid.
107   A Special Jury could be asked for by the plaintiff for a fee. It was chosen from men of a particular class or rank in society. They were often used where a case was complicated and it was felt that members of the jury needed to be educated.

Susan Bartlett, who had been a servant to William Stickland for eleven years, declared that she had often been present when the plaintiff and the defendant had discussed marriage and had heard him say many times that he would not marry her, to which Wilhelmina replied many times that she did not ask him to. George Stone, a labourer living in Beaminster, claimed he overheard a conversation between Wilhelmina and William about his impending marriage to Miss Paul. According to him, Wilhelmina said that she would let the world know that she had a claim on him. He also heard her say that she had no letters or writings from him, as he was always so close to her that writing was not necessary.

What letters there were, including the one where William promised marriage, were presented to the judge for inspection, which he did with the aid of a magnifying glass. In his summing up Justice Biles referred to the letters, which appeared to him to have been touched up in places and rewritten in parts, something he thought the jury might like to take into account when considering their verdict. Despite this, there was, in his view, sufficient verbal evidence to substantiate a claim. The jury could not agree immediately so retired to consult. They returned with a verdict in favour of Wilhelmina and awarded her £150 damages. She spent the rest of her life as a spinster, living with her family and dying at the age of 59. Her son became a cabinet maker, married and lived in London. William and his wife settled down in Allington, Bridport.

***

William Charles Lambert was a barrister of the Middle Temple, described as a man of amiable temper, possessed of a competent fortune and husband of a woman selected with the most fervent and sincere passion that perhaps ever warmed the breast of a man. The woman he chose as his wife was Georgiana Charlotte Norcott, daughter of Maj Gen Sir Amos Norcott, who led his regiment at the Battle of Waterloo and became Lieutenant Governor of Jamaica. The couple married on 31 July 1829 in Cheltenham and after living in London for a short period they embarked on a tour of the Continent. On their return they lived in Weymouth for a while before looking for a house in Dorset, suitable to their wealth and status. The property they chose was Knowle, a house just outside Wimborne, which they moved into in 1832. Georgina's uncle, Mr Cunningham-Taylor, visited them on several occasions

William Hanham in his naval captain's uniform. William served in the Caribbean and was also an officer in the Dorset Yeomanry. (Copyright Sir William Hanham.)

and thought them a happy and loving couple.

Being a native of Dorset, William was no stranger to the gentlemen of the county and soon he and his wife were mingling in the upper circles of local society. One such was a gentleman named William Hanham who lived at High Hall, Wimborne, whom they met through local acquaintances.

One of those acquaintances was a Mr Coventry who invited William Hanham and the Lamberts to a dinner party on 8 January 1833. During the meal the setting up of a shooting party was discussed and it was agreed that one would be held the following day. Next morning William Lambert left his wife at home to go on the shoot and what happened next was described by several witnesses, including servants and men who were working in the grounds.

William Smith was a blacksmith who, whilst working on a dovecote at Knowle that morning, observed Mrs Lambert walking along the carriage way when Mr Hanham arrived on a small pony. Instead of riding up to the house, where a servant would take the horse, he rode up to Mrs Lambert, dismounted and held the bridle with his left hand, taking the lady's arm just above the wrist with the other. Smith then saw them go into a plantation towards the summer house, which was secluded. The couple were next seen two hours

later, emerging from the plantation but not arm in arm. Hanham then went into the house and left 15 minutes later. During his visit he extended a dinner invitation to the Lamberts at his house. They had dined with him several times at High Hall, but this was the first time they were to stay overnight.

High Hall, Wimborne, scene of the marital drama involving Georgiana Lambert, her husband and William Hanham. (cc-by-sa/2.0-Furzehill: High Hall by Chris Downer-geograph.org.uk/p/10672.)

On the said day, the guests assembled at 5 pm and after dinner some of the party went home and others stayed. Unusually, Mrs Lambert had not brought her maid with her, so the maid of a Mrs Loftus, called Mary Hill, attended her and made up the bed. It was gone midnight when Mrs Loftus left the drawing room, followed a few minutes later by Mrs Lambert. Mrs Loftus had been in bed for about half an hour when she heard something she described as a slight rustling, as though someone had passed outside her door in the passage. She was dozing off when she heard a more violent noise, like someone bursting open a door. She told her husband to investigate but he said it was only drunken servants going to bed. Then she heard voices and dreadful sounds, such as groans and someone struggling. Mr Loftus finally put on his dressing gown and linen drawers and went to investigate. Almost immediately he heard William Lambert's voice crying out loudly, 'Loftus! Loftus come here – come to me; oh God what have I seen; we are separated for ever.' Mrs Loftus' maid said that she heard a man's voice, the scream of a woman and a heavy noise, as if someone had fallen. This was followed by a man's voice crying out, 'Where is he? Where is he? The villain's fled – I threw a bottle at him – The rascal! I'll murder him – As to her, poor creature, I'll leave her – Oh, my God! Oh, my God! What have I seen? Loftus! Loftus – I've been listening at the door for nearly an hour.'[108] As for Mrs Lambert, she dashed into the Loftus' room in a state of great distress and crying, wearing her dressing gown but no slippers. After being calmed, instead of returning to her room, she spent the night downstairs in the drawing room. The next morning Mrs Lambert asked Mrs Loftus' maid to retrieve one of her slippers from Hanham's room, which was found by the washstand.

Mr Oglander was another guest, who hearing the ruckus came out of his room that night. He observed William Hanham on the landing, leaning on the bannister of the staircase, with a wound to his head. Hanham then disappeared and went to hide somewhere in the house. He was not seen again that night and next morning he left with Oglander and went to Ringwood.

William Lambert brought a case of Criminal Conversation against William Hanham, held at the summer assizes in 1833. In such cases a husband was entitled to sue another party for having sexual relations with his wife and claim damages. The case, which aroused great interest among the gentry of Dorset, to the degree that they filled the public gallery, was before a Special Jury. After listening to the testimony of the various witnesses

---

108   *Chronicle* 25/7/1833.

it was time for Sir James Scarlett,[109] lead lawyer for the defence, to take to the floor. He was one of the most successful advocates of the time and thought to be particularly effective before a jury. He called no witnesses but gave a long eloquent speech claiming that despite the circumstantial evidence there was not a scrap of proof that anything untoward had taken place between Georgiana Lambert and William Hanham. In his submission he related his client's version of what happened on that night at High Hall. According to Hanham, after his guests had gone their various ways he had retired to his library to write a letter and after completing it went up to his bedroom, where he was accustomed to read before sleeping. He had been in bed for several minutes when he realised that he needed to go downstairs again and opened the door to do so. On the stairs he saw a lady in her dressing gown and so, being a gentleman, he went to go back into his room. But, before he could do so, Mrs Lambert was pushed into his room and he was attacked violently with a glass by her husband, causing a severe wound.

Georgiana did not appear at the trial but her version of what happened was put in a letter to Sir James Scarlett. She stated that she retired to her room at about 12.30 and decided to repair some lace on her bonnet. Her husband came up about half an hour afterwards. Then she had occasion to go downstairs, where she remained for about ten minutes and on her return she was surprised to see her bedroom door wide open. Immediately, her husband appeared and, placing one hand around her throat and drawing the other down her face, he exclaimed, 'We are parted for ever'. The violence he used forced her into Hanham's room, the door of which was partially open, and once in there her husband began attacking him as he tried to intervene. She ran into her own room, fearing for her life, and hid under the bed and when things had quietened down a little she hurried to Mrs Loftus' room to seek her protection, thinking her husband to be intoxicated or mentally deranged.

Having heard all the evidence and the pleas, the judge retired the court to his lodgings where the jury were to deliberate. After about half an hour they gave their verdict in favour of the defendant, Hanham. It was then that the judge told them that the plaintiff had anticipated the result and consented to be non-suited and consequently the case was withdrawn. This meant that after all the airing of dirty laundry none benefitted, save the lawyers. Sir James Scarlett received 600 guineas for his trouble, worth about £80,000 today.

---

109   Sir James Scarlett, 1st Baron Abinger (1769–1844). Politician as well as lawyer, he was guardian to the father of the poet Elizabeth Barrett Browning.

With William Hanham exonerated the Lamberts went on to battle it out between themselves. In the Consistory Court,[110] Georgiana put in a claim for the restitution of conjugal rights – conjugal rights meaning her entitlement as a spouse to be, among other things, maintained by her husband. She also claimed that he had committed adultery, but could provide no evidence. In his counter claim William said that his wife had committed adultery twice in Weymouth, including with a major of the dragoon guards, and had also been intimate with the Earl of M [sic], who they had become friendly with in Florence whilst on the Grand Tour. He declared that after they had returned home she had written letters to the Earl clandestinely and he provided the court with an extract from one of them. She had supposedly written, 'In mercy burn this, for I tremble and fear discovery. Think sometimes of your absent and fond love. Again, God bless you. Don't dearest M ever forget me; and feel assured of my love.'[111] The court pronounced against Georgiana and said that her husband was entitled to a divorce. William threw his wife out of the marital home, forbidding her to return. He declared that she had destroyed the ties that existed between man and wife and was unfit to be again admitted to his house.

The next time William was involved in litigation it was in a Sheriff's Court where he sued a Mr W C Mitchell for using his name. Mitchell had assumed his name because he was cohabitating with Georgina in Hampstead and she was pregnant by him. William was claimed damages of £3,000, but because he had banished his wife he was only awarded £100. The couple finally divorced in 1835 and both remarried. Georgiana became not Mrs Mitchell but Mrs Theodald and lived in Hounslow, where she became a noted sportswoman. She was killed in 1845 when she fell off her horse.

William married Agnes Grove Helyar in 1844 and made his home at Steepleton Manor, Winterbourne Steepleton, Dorset. He became a magistrate and served on the Dorset grand jury.

***

Mary Boatswain, on bail, surrendered herself on the charge of wilfully taking poison at Abbotsbury on 12 January 1873, intending to kill herself. She was described as a good-looking young woman. She confessed to the crime and

---

110   A type of ecclesiastical court, especially in the Church of England.
111   *Chronicle* 22/5/1834.

seemed to be very penitent. Mary said that she had fallen in love and written a letter intended to be read after the poison had done its work. She had taken a large quantity of alcohol followed by rat poison. Fortunately, someone called the village doctor, Dr Boreham, who administered the necessary antidotes, which saved her life. She was found guilty by the jury but the judge took a lenient view, sentencing her to one day in prison. He added that he hoped not to see her in court again. Mary never appeared at an assize court again but she did appear before a magistrates' court a year later.

One of the occupations for the women in the village of Abbotsbury was that of 'Breeder of fishing nets'. Their job was to make and repair the fishing nets that were used by the men of the village who fished off Chesil Beach. Three women who were employed doing this lived in Back Street. Hannah Ford, aged 38, lived next door to Elizabeth Gee, aged 50, and living a couple of doors away from her was Mary Boatswain, aged 25. At the county petty sessions held in May 1874 the three women appeared, together with George Boatswain, Mary's father, to sort out what the *Southern Times* termed 'a woman's matter and a general scrimmage', [112] during which George's mother and Mary were knocked down and Hannah Ford and her mother fell upon them. This provoked George into saying that if the Fords did not leave his family alone he would strike them. His threat was disregarded and it was alleged that he struck Hannah Ford on the head and she was 'all of a gore of blood'. George denied the assault, but that was not the end of the matter. In a second case, Hannah Ford was said to have knocked Mary Boatswain down and held her by the neck. The parties were bound over to keep the peace for three months. These were acts one and two of a three-part drama, because Hannah Ford was summoned for assaulting Elizabeth Gee. It was alleged that she came to Gee's door, and after abusing her threw a stone at her, hitting her on the head. Hannah was fined ten shillings.

The newspapers reporting the cases gave no indication of the cause of Mary's intended suicide or the animosity between the families, but there is one small clue that might suggest what might have been at the centre of it all. Sometime in the last quarter of 1875 Mary Boatswain gave birth to a son, Henry George Ford Boatswain. The birth entry indicates that she was unmarried, but the significant thing, of course, is that he was given the name Ford, most probably the surname of the father.

Mary was back in court in May 1880, this time as the prosecutrix, [113] accusing Charles Cleall of stealing a basket of mackerel from her at Weymouth

---

112   *Southern Times* 16/5/1874.
113   A female prosecutor.

railway station. Cleall, who was worse for drink at the time, denied taking the fish and the magistrate pointed out that there was heavy traffic in mackerel that day and some of the baskets might have got mixed up. Fearing that the case might be referred to the assizes, Cleall asked for the matter to be dealt with summarily and agreed to pay a fine of five shillings, plus costs. Mary remained living with her parents until 1886, when she married Solomon Saunders.

***

In the first half of the nineteenth century roads were being improved by engineers like John McAdam, but the most efficient way of moving heavy goods in Britain was through coastal trade. Originally done by sailing craft, with the advent of the steam engine the steam packet was coming into its own. It was generally faster than sail and did not have to rely on wind direction. Charles Butt was the captain and owner of such a craft, plying his trade between Exeter and London. In June 1839 his ship lay up in Weymouth and it was whilst he was there that he made the acquaintance of Jane Winter. Jane kept an inn in the town, The Old Rooms, on the quay.[114]

She was a young bride at nineteen and widowed at twenty seven, leaving her with two daughters to bring up. The *Salisbury Journal* described Jane as 'buxom and gay, and the hostess of a house in a thriving business – ready money at her command, and altogether not an unenviable helpmate'.[115] These attractions were not lost on Mr Butt, who 'shortly after the introduction began to make desperate love to the widow, who returned his affections with great

The Old Rooms, by Weymouth Quay, were established in 1771. In 1839 they were owned by Jane Winter. (Author copyright.)

114   The Old Rooms is still a popular pub.
115   *Salisbury Journal* 15/3/1841.

ardour'.[116] The relationship grew and Ann Beal, a relative of Jane, deposed in court that the couple appeared to be very fond of each other. The packet captain decided to declare his intentions to Jane in a letter. He wrote, 'I am truly unhappy respecting the bill [debt] I have to meet on a friend who will take legal proceedings against me … which, my dear, will be injurious to you and your dear children whom I have the greatest regard for, for there is not a person in Weymouth I would be under the obligation to, excepting yourself to ask them for a shilling. My dear I am short of five pounds and if you will oblige me with a loan I shall be forever under an obligation to you and prove myself an affectionate husband and loving father. I am anxious to have the result of this note. By doing so you will for ever oblige your constant lover until death.'[117]

Despite the questionable motive for Butt's love the courtship flourished, and there came a point when people noticed that Jane was becoming a little rotund around the waist, leading them to believe that as she was a respectable woman the couple had married secretly and were going to make an addition to their family. However, they had not wed, so the two of them visited Jane's solicitor to get him to draw up a marriage settlement. Given her condition it was decided that they ought to wed, but not in Weymouth, feeling that there was no point in dispelling the belief that they had already been through a wedding ceremony. Accordingly, Charles went to Halstock, where Jane had some property, to get the Banns read, and it was from there that he wrote another letter to her, saying that he could not get the banns read because he did not belong to that parish and that he was going to London for a week. Jane heard nothing more from Capt. Butt for several months and, in his absence, she gave birth to his son. When she did hear news of him it was to be told that he had married a rich woman and could be seen riding around Weymouth in his gig. Her next action was to initiate proceedings for compensation in the court of Nisi Prius.

Butt's plea was that he had made no promises of marriage, and if he did, they were rescinded by mutual consent. He accused Jane of being an immodest and lewd person. After taking into account the letters that were written and the fact that the two were living together the jury sided with Jane and awarded her damages of £100.

***

116   Ibid.
117   Ibid.

Legal counsel prided themselves on their oratory skills, and cases involving marital affairs gave them a good opportunity to exercise them. Such was the case of Slade vs Furnell. Robert Slade was suing Henry Knight Furnell for criminal conversation with his wife, in the sum of £3,000. Slade was a successful Newfoundland merchant, a Poole councillor and one-time Sheriff of the borough, who lived in the area of St James. Furnell, also from Poole, was an iron merchant. Both men were married. Thirty-five-year-old Slade married his wife Sarah Gardiner, who was about the same age as him, in 1817 and they had five children aged three to thirteen at the time of the court case. Furnell, aged thirty-two, had been married to his wife Elizabeth for five years and also had children.

Serjeant Wilde opened the case for the plaintiff, which was one that according to the newspapers aroused considerable interest. Wilde stated that Furnell had 'deprived Robert Slade of the affections of a wife, and his children of the attentions of a parent, thus rendering asunder those ties and feelings which are the only source of domestic happiness',[118] and that 'If ever a man came into court with a case of this nature, under circumstances of greater aggravation, or which called for more severe reprobation of the conduct of the defendant than another, the plaintiff was the man'. He pushed home his point, continuing with, 'I will not try, for the power of language is inadequate, and if it were not so, I should ill occupy the time of the jury, were I to attempt the task of dilating on the distress which must fall so overpoweringly on a man who has five children left without a mother'.[119] Wilde then went on to explain the type of case that this one was not, when he proclaimed that, 'Marriages were frequently contracted between persons of unequal ages, or whose dispositions did not harmonize together; or the defendant may have proceeded under circumstances of great temptation; he might have seen youth and beauty pining under ill usage, and appealing with the silent magic to the human feelings of human nature; he might have pitied, then admired, and allowed the passion to grow upon him, until without being aware of its force, he might in an unguarded moment have been hurried into an excess of which he must repent when it was too late.'[120] No, this was a case 'where the defendant had no acquaintance with Mrs Slade, until he sought it for the criminal prosecution of his purposes'. Sarah Slade was described as 'pure and uncontaminated by crime',[121] who

---

118   *Chronicle* 18/3/1830.
119   Ibid.
120   Ibid.
121   Ibid.

had been forced to leave the family home and was now living with her mother.

To support these charges several witnesses were called, mostly servants of the Slade family. The first was Jane Lockyer, their nursemaid, who had been with the family for about four months. She confirmed that Mr and Mrs Slade kept themselves to themselves and rarely visited other people, and that the husband was particularly devoted to his wife. As part of her duties the nursemaid often accompanied Mrs Slade on her walks with the children. Then, one day, they were joined by a man, whom she confirmed was Mr Furnell, who walked with them for about two hours. The next day he joined them again, her mistress walking ahead whilst she walked behind with the children. The walks became more frequent, about four or five times a week, each time being accompanied by the stranger. Jane thought that the couple were getting more familiar with each other, until, on one of the walks, she was shocked and embarrassed when he kissed Sarah Slade. So shocked was the nursemaid that she felt it incumbent to mention the incident to her mistress. On another occasion, Mrs Slade interrupted their walk and told Jane to take the children into town to buy them some cakes, leaving her alone with the defendant. As instructed, she took the children into town, but did not rejoin her mistress, taking them home instead.

On Sundays Robert Slade went regularly to church and, at the same time, Furnell became a regular visitor to the Slade house, always arriving after her husband left. The nursemaid then told of a change in Sarah's behaviour. On occasions she had found her mistress intoxicated, something she had never seen until Furnell began to visit her.

It seems that the visits by Furnell to the Slade household were not confined to Sundays. According to Rachel Silcox, another servant, her mistress entertained Furnell four or five times a week whilst her husband was at work. She then went on to describe what she had witnessed on a number of occasions. 'I have seen Mr Furnell and my mistress go into the best bedroom often, about ten times, and have the door locked, where they remained for about twenty minutes. I have gone into the bedroom after they have left it, and saw that the bed appeared to be tumbled, as if someone had been lying in it.'[122]

Robert was slow to catch on about what was going on under his roof, but eventually his suspicions were aroused and he challenged Furnell over it in a letter, setting out occasions the accused had more than casual meetings

---

122   Ibid.

with his wife. Furnell's reply was then read out in court. In it he assured
Slade that nothing untoward had happened between him and Sarah. He had
occasionally walked with her, always accompanied by his children and the
nursemaid. No mention was made of any visits to the house. Finally, Furnell
said he regretted exceedingly that any improper motive should have been
attributed to his conduct, and that the uneasiness in Robert's mind was felt
equally in his. Lastly, he assured him that no meetings would take place
again. Whatever his intentions, Furnell continued to meet Sarah, which led
to the action in the court in March 1830.

It was now time for Wilde to go back into actor mode, taking advantage
of the fact that all the jury were men, the majority of whom were probably
married. Addressing them directly, he said, 'In cases such of this kind, it
was customary to talk of compensation; but such a word was inapplicable;
it was indeed, some consolation to the plaintiff to receive the sympathy of
his fellow men, to know that they felt for his situation and commiserated
for his loss; but to talk of a sum of money as a compensation to a man who
had just buried all his hopes of domestic happiness, who has been deprived
of the affections of a wife, whose children have become motherless, whose
home has been a desert, was utterly an anomaly.'[123] Finally he emphasised
that 'this was a case of a virtuous, estimable woman, whom it had taken
years of attention to seduce, by youth and all that can charm and fascinate a
female'.[124] Defence counsel were now going to show this was not the case by
blackening Sarah's character.

The first witness for the defence was Mrs Slade's cousin Charlotte Sellers,
who told the court that five years earlier, whilst walking out with Sarah on
the Wimborne to Ringwood road, they met two men who appeared to be
army officers. She contended that one of them kissed her cousin, and when
she suggested that her husband would be offended Sarah replied that he
would not know. She then went on to say that her cousin thought the two
officers handsome and that she would like to meet them one evening, and
if she did would Charlotte go with her? She declined the offer but inferred
that Sarah did go. On another occasion, Sarah was in the garden watering
flowers when the two officers passed by. She supposedly commented that she
would have liked to invite them into her house if her husband were not at
home. Further accusations were made by the cousin, including an occasion
when she overheard Sarah talking to a young man and suggesting they meet
in the churchyard, but he said it was too damp. Charlotte did not know the

123   Ibid.
124   Ibid.

purpose of the meeting. She also confirmed that Mr Slade had complained of his wife's drunkenness.

Anna Maria Sellers, sister to Charlotte, pronounced a whole list of occasions when Sarah either met men who kissed her hand or expressed a wish to meet them; she also said that she had witnessed Sarah so drunk she could hardly stand. One accusation she made was that Sarah had gone to a local druggist to buy some love powder to make men admire her more by putting it into their drink.

A Sarah Smith, who said she knew Mrs Slade, added to the case against her. 'I have seen her take the hat off Peter Froud, one of her servants and run away with it; I have also seen her pull his clothes, and take off his neck clothe; Froud on these occasions kissed her; I have seen him, on one occasion, take her in his arms, and heard her exclaim, "Oh God, Peter, don't squeeze me so hard". He would then let her go and they would run up the garden. I have seen her jump on his back.' At a time when a woman's role was clearly defined and her behaviour constantly under observation, if these assertions were true Sarah's behaviour was scandalous.

Nothing was said by the defence about Sarah's behaviour with Furnell, save a statement from John Leaf, who worked for the defendant and noticed that every time she passed the window of his employer's premises she stood on tip-toe and looked into the window.

The witnesses in this duel having completed their evidence, it was now time for Serjeant Wilde to present his finale to the jury, telling them that, 'The unfeeling murderers of private happiness did not stop until they had attempted to destroy the peace of mind of all connected with their victims, by further injuring the character of the wife. … If she had been a wife of some weakness, she was at least one of honour. He has defiled the bed of her husband and rioted in it to excess. He has arrayed up all her crimes, dragged her from the bosom of her family, and caused her to be published to the whole town of Poole, as one so degraded and vile that to look on her is pollution.'[125]

Finally, the jury retired to consider their verdict, and on their return found for Robert Slade and awarded damages of £400.

In November following the case in Dorchester another cause was held, this time in an Ecclesiastical Court at Canford, Poole. The suit was instituted by Robert against Sarah for a divorce *mensa et thoro*, a phrase that means a divorce from bed and board. Such a divorce is more like a legal separation,

125   Ibid.

where the husband and wife are not legally obliged to live together, but their marriage has not been dissolved. Robert and Sarah did not live together again. As for Henry Furnell, he returned to his wife and family and they are shown as still living together forty years later.

Child Offenders

At a time when alcohol was the main liquid refreshment of the poor, there were numerous cases of crime being caused by excessive drinking. Most were minor and dealt with by the magistrates, but on occasions the result was more serious and had to be dealt with by the assize judges. Most raised little interest, but one case, heard in July 1847, filled the court with curious spectators. It was a charge of grievous bodily harm, committed by James Hayward, aged just 10. The prosecutor in the case was his victim, 13-year-old George Elkins.

The two boys had been drinking at a public house called The Chops, in Blandford, when a quarrel broke out between the two and escalated into what one witness referred to as 'shocking language'.[126] The argument carried on outside and at some point Hayward struck Elkins with a laurel bough and Elkins reciprocated, hitting the other boy a couple of times with a stick. Then Hayward took a clasp knife from his pocket and opened it saying, 'I'll stick this into you',[127] and stabbed him in the left side. The wounded boy was taken immediately to a neighbour, where he was examined by a doctor who reported that the knife had penetrated between the fifth and sixth rib, causing a life-threatening injury. Elkins' condition remained serious for a week, during which he had an attack of pleurisy. In the court the 10-year-old prisoner had to answer questions from a barrister but had no one representing him. The absurdity of this situation was magnified when Judge Williams was required to ask the child if there were any questions he wished to ask the witnesses or if he wanted to address the jury in his defence. Not surprisingly the answer was in the negative. After the jury found James guilty of common assault the judge declared that he did not know what to do with him, and deferred sentence until the next day, when he was given a prison sentence of three months. Reporting on the case, the *Hull Advertiser* described it as displaying a shocking picture of youthful depravity.[128]

James' short time in prison at such a young age might have put him off crime for life, but the contrary was true. At the age of 17 he was convicted of stealing a silk handkerchief, a favourite of pickpockets because they always fetched a good price. For that he was imprisoned for one year with hard

---

126 *Salisbury Journal* 24/7/1847.
127 Ibid.
128 *Hull Advertiser* 30/7/1847.

labour. Then, two years later, he had a month in jail for poaching. In that same year James married a local girl, Salina Stanley, got a job as a chimney sweep, and it appeared that at last he had settled down. And he did, that is until 1878, when he appeared at the Dorset Sessions, this time for obtaining a purse containing four sovereigns and a four-penny piece belonging to Fanny Castleman. That appeared to be James' last criminal act. He resumed his employment as a sweep and he and Salina lived in Blandford until her death in 1891. He was now 53 and ready to marry again. A year after his wife's death he wed the 28-year old Emily Brown, with whom he remained until his death in 1901.

***

Had James Hayward felt able to address the jury at his trial he might have been able to convince them that he stabbed George Elkins in self-defence. In another prosecution, that of Charles Edmonds, there was little chance of that happening, as his motives and actions were very clear. Charles, aged 14, was indicted on the serious charge of 'unlawfully, maliciously, and feloniously wounding one Sarah Tizzard, with intent then and there to kill and murder her, at Child Okeford, Dorset, on 10th December, 1880'.[129]

As head servant at Hayward Lodge, the property of widow Maria Harvey, Sarah Tizzard had her work cut out. The house included three reception rooms, a library, ten bedrooms, dressing rooms and a large kitchen. Outside there were extensive lawns, plus flower beds, a kitchen garden and a grass tennis court, all tended by Walter Ames, the 71-year-old gardener. Sarah, aged 39, was an experienced servant and when her mistress went away from the house she had no hesitation in leaving it in her charge, which she had occasion to do in December 1880.

On the previous 24 October Sarah noticed that some money was missing from her purse. Suspecting that another employee, Charles Edmonds, a 14-year-old labourer, had taken it she asked him outright if he had. The boy denied it and Sarah said to him, 'If you won't tell me you shall know the consequences'. He said, 'You won't tell Ames, will you?' to which she replied, 'Not if you bring it back'. There was an impasse between the two of them until 10 December when Edmonds presented three shillings to her,

---

129   Dorset Calendar of Prisoners.

which prompted Sarah to say, 'Charlie, you will bring back the rest of the money, won't you? It's near Christmas and I want to buy some things'.[130]

That evening Sarah was alone in the kitchen when she heard the sound of gravel hitting the window, followed by someone outside calling her name. She recognised that it was Charles and let him in, surprised to see that he was carrying two iron bars, of which the smaller one he brought into the house. Sarah followed the boy into the kitchen and there was some conversation about mending some slippers. Sarah asked him what the iron bar was for and Charles replied that his father said it would be good to put the slipper on when repairing it. His manner and the fact that he had not sat down was making Sarah feel uneasy, so she went and stood by the dresser, at which point the boy put the iron bar on his shoulder. The maid was becoming concerned and asked, 'Charlie, what did you do that for?'[131] Instead of answering her question Charles did something that must have brought terror into her mind. He calmly walked over to the kitchen door and locked it. Her worst fears were realised when the boy approached and struck her with the bar on the left side of the head, stunning her. Struggling to get to the kitchen door, Sarah fell by a store cupboard and looking round saw her attacker looking for a knife in a drawer. He found one and came towards her with it as she was trying to get up to leave the kitchen. Advancing towards her, Charles said, 'Do you think I can't manage you?'[132] Things were becoming desperate, but Sarah did manage to get the door open and went into the passage, followed by Charles, who came up behind her, put his arms around her and stuffed something she could not identify into her mouth. Her assailant still had the crowbar in his hand and started beating her with it again, until she fell to the floor. She told the court that she could feel the pain and started to scream until a hand was put over her face. Then the drama took a bizarre twist. Suddenly, the boy cried out, 'Oh, my head', and Sarah said, 'What is the matter Charlie, did I strike you, I never intended to?' Charles replied that he realised that he had always loved her and did what he did for fear of her telling his father that he had stolen her money, even though he had not done so. Sarah assured him that she would not have told anyone, and she certainly did not deserve the treatment she had received from him. Things had calmed down now between the two parties and Charles had to think of a way out of a difficult situation. He suggested that they should tell Ames and his boss that some

130   *Salisbury Journal* 29/1/1881.
131   Ibid.
132   Ibid

'big fellow' had been in and nearly killed them both. Eventually he made Sarah swear she would not tell anybody of what had happened.

Even if Sarah had sworn not to tell, she had several obvious injuries to her head that needed treatment which would provoke questions from a doctor as to how she had got them. It was local doctor Decimus Curme who was called out that night to attend to the servant. He attested that when he arrived at Hayward Lodge he found her in an excited state and with twelve wounds on her head and face, some of which were serious. Police constable Vatcher, in his evidence to the court, described how when he charged Charles, the boy said, 'I know I done it; but if you let me off now I won't do it any more',[133] a statement that raises a question about the young boy's moral awareness.

Mr Lock, defending Charles, appealed to the jury to temper justice with mercy, which he contended was one of the cardinal points of English law. He also pointed them towards the character reference given by Rev. J.G. Brymer, the rector of Child Okeford, who declared that he had known the prisoner for nearly seven years and was not aware of anything against him, describing the boy as excessively quiet. Inevitably, the judge, Justice Lopes, asked Brymer if he had noticed anything strange about Charles' mental condition. He answered in the negative but added that he had found it difficult to teach Charles certain subjects, such as arithmetic. Here the judge intervened, adding a little levity to the proceedings by saying, 'That would not show any disease of the mind – if so there would be a good many people of diseased minds'.[134] In summing up he said that the jury would doubtless pay attention to the weapon used and the degree of the wounds when they considered the motive of the accused. He added that it was a mad case and one he deeply regretted. The jury found Charles guilty of a lesser charge of wounding with intent to cause bodily harm and recommended leniency, because of his age. He was sentenced to one month in prison, to be followed by five years confinement in a reformatory for young people.[135]

⁕⁕⁕

---

133   Ibid.
134   Ibid.
135   See page 97.

Fire and matches have always fascinated children and many of us have taken delight in making a small fire or lighting a bonfire on Guy Fawkes Night, but occasionally things can get out of hand.

On 14 September 1858 Frederick Foot was digging potatoes on his allotment in the village of Dewlish, seven miles north-west of Dorchester, when he noticed smoke from a field known as 'Pitfield Bottom'. The fire was coming from a barley stack owned by farmer Joseph Squibb. Running towards the stack he was just in time to see a local boy, John Cross, running away. Foot chased the boy and when he caught up with him he said, 'You young rascal, what have you been doing? You will be sure to be hung,'[136] to which the boy replied, 'I did that'. Foot then let the boy go and went to tell the farmer what had happened. Stephen Cutler was the village constable who went looking for John, but when the boy saw him he ran off, with the policeman in pursuit. After about half a mile the boy jumped into a stream but was secured and dragged onto the bank where Cutler asked him what he had done. The two of them must have known each other pretty well, because John answered using the man's first name, saying, 'I hope, Stephen, you will forgive me this time'.[137] Farmer Squibb brought John, aged 11, before the magistrate, Rev. J.A. Templer, who committed him for trial at the next assizes. The following March the boy appeared before the jury and was found guilty, with a recommendation for mercy because they did not believe he was in possession of all his faculties. The judge was similarly minded and sentenced him to a month imprisonment, followed by five years at a reformatory. In the Dorchester gaol admissions register it is noted that the 11-year-old was employed as a labourer at the time of the crime.

***

Harry Parker was another child incendiary. Standing in the dock at the 1873 Lent assizes, his curly red hair could only just be seen above the rail of the dock. Harry was just 7 years old and indicted with feloniously setting fire to a stable, a crime punishable by a life sentence. The prosecutrix was Mrs Jane Ballard who claimed that Harry had burned down her stable at West Walls, Wareham. Harry pleaded guilty to the offence, so without further ado it was up to the judge, Justice Grove, to decide what to do with him. Taking

---

136 *Southern Times* 25/9/1858.
137 Ibid.

into account the age of the boy, he said that he was of a mind to send him to a reformatory school. He told Harry that he was anxious to prevent him growing wild and getting into bad company. He therefore sentenced him to ten days in prison, followed by five years detention in a reformatory.

***

The mother of Elizabeth Mellish was either completely devoid of any feeling for her child or very clever. Eleven-year-old Elizabeth was brought to the bar of the court for stealing a hare on 13 February 1845 from the house of William Bligdon, a blacksmith from Litton Cheney. The young girl was a sorry sight in court, described as being poor-looking and half starved. When the charge was put to her and she was asked to plead, the little creature replied, 'Guilty'. When Justice Erle asked her if she knew what she was doing she replied, 'Yes', but the judge was not convinced and enquired whether she had received any advice or been visited in gaol by anybody, to which she said that she had not. She was then asked if she had stolen the hare and she said that she had. Erle decided that Elizabeth was too young to exercise discretion and suggested that she change her plea to not guilty, which she did.

The principal witness for the prosecution was Mrs Bligdon, who deposed that on the day in question she left her house, leaving the door open, and when she returned she found that a hare was missing. Someone must have seen Elizabeth going into or leaving the house, because as a consequence of their information the blacksmith's wife set off after the young girl, accompanied by a constable. Eventually they caught up with the alleged offender who was walking with her mother and carrying something on her head, which turned out to be part of a hare wrapped up in some of her mother's belongings. On being asked if she had stolen the hare Elizabeth burst into tears and said she had done so to pay for lodgings, because her father had beaten them both and thrown them out of the house. The mother denied knowing anything about the affair.

In his summing up, Justice Erle advised the jury that there was great doubt whether the child acted alone or under the influence of her mother. Elizabeth was found not guilty. The question arises as to whether Elizabeth's mother's denial was a blatant attempt to blame her daughter, or if her thinking was that if her daughter was charged she would be likely to get off because of her age.

***

At the 1835 Dorset assize, Justice Patterson took the opportunity to inform the grand jury of his thoughts on reducing child crime among the lower classes. He applauded that much had been done to give a 'better tone of mind' to the lower classes by the spread of Christian education, but then went on to say that he did not mean mere reading and writing; because simply teaching these was putting power into the hands of the people, which might be turned to good or evil. Clearly, Patterson felt that knowledge could be a dangerous thing in the hands of the lower orders. In fact, the good judge had done a little research on this subject and found that out of 38 cases set down before him that day, more than two-thirds of the accused could read or write, showing that it did not necessarily follow that because a person could read or write that they were good members of society.

At another assize, Justice Crowther in his charge to the grand jury specifically referred to juvenile delinquency in Dorset and he too had done a little research. He told them that in the previous seven years, 324 persons had been admitted to prison under the age of 16 years. Of these, 19 were under the age of 9 years, 44 between 9 and 12, and 261 between 12 and 16. He then congratulated the authorities in the county for their determination to establish reformatories, under a recent act of Parliament, and hoped that they would be effective in reducing child crime.

The nineteenth century saw a change in attitude to the punishment of young criminals, with an emphasis away from the notion of serving time in a prison to that of having an element of reform, in the hope that offenders might be taken off the path to more serious crimes. In 1846 Lord Houghton attempted to introduce a bill into Parliament that would establish a reformatory school system, and although it did not pass, it did arouse interest in the idea. A number of voluntary schools were established, but it was the Reformatory School Act of 1854, and another in 1857, that formalised arrangements. The voluntary schools had to be certified by the Inspector of Prisons and convicted offenders below the age of 16 could be pardoned on condition they were committed to a reform school for a period of between two to five years. By 1875 there were 54 certified reform schools in England and Wales.

A leading light in the reformatory movement in Dorset was John Mansel-Pleydell, a major landowner in the county. Among his many interests he was attracted to the problem of juvenile crime and in 1857 he built a reformatory school in the village of Milborne St Andrew, situated nine miles north-east of Dorchester. The school took 24 boys and the emphasis was on education, particularly religious education, and on the development of skill that would enable them to get work. Twenty-four years after its inception, the establishment changed its role to that of an Industrial School, helping homeless boys. A reformatory school for girls also existed in Poole.

Suffer the Little Children – Child Cruelty

The predominant image of child labour in the nineteenth century is that of the dark satanic mills, mentioned in William Blake's poem 'And Did Those Feet in Ancient Time', with children working 13-hour days in dangerous and unhealthy conditions. Many of them came from the Union workhouses, which were convenient sources of labour and places where once a child was placed there was little checking up on their condition. Of course, it was not just the factories that had an appetite for child labour. There was also a market for servants and apprentices, and children placed with masters and mistresses were no less open to danger and abuse than those in the factories, as the following two cases show.

In 1853 the *Southern Times* carried the following article headline – 'ATROCIOUS CRUELTY TO A POOR FATHERLESS BOY' – and went on to give details of an inquest held in the Three Cups Hotel, Lyme Regis. Matthew Leno had spent much of his young life in the workhouse at Axminster in Devon, until at the age of 14 he was sent by the Guardians to

A child sweep. (Courtesy of the Wellcome Collection, attribution 4.0 international [CC BY 4.0].)

work with a chimney sweep named Swain in Honiton. After just five weeks he ran away, back to his mother Priscilla, who lived in Lyme Regis. But she was in no position to support him so decided to return him to the workhouse, which in turn put him for a probationary period with a Bridport sweep named William Green. Matthew had worked for Green for about three weeks when the sweep took the boy to his mother and entered into an agreement for him to be apprenticed. The mother told Green that if he misbehaved he should discipline him as a father would, something she would live to regret saying.

Priscilla heard nothing more of her son until five weeks had passed, when a Mr Jackson sent for her to collect her son, who was staying at his house. She must have been appalled when she saw her boy. When he last left her, he looked perfectly healthy, but now he was unable to walk and had bad chilblains and dropsy. The skin on his back and thigh was all sorts of colours, red, black and green, indicating that he had been flogged. Mrs Leno then picked Matthew up and carried him home. Dr Cary was summoned, who was told by Matthew that he had been unable to walk for a fortnight, and that the sweep had used him mercilessly, to the extent that Green's wife had asked him to stop his harsh behaviour. The poor boy was with his mother for seven days before he breathed his last breath and left a world that for him contained nothing but poverty and misery.

Giving evidence, Dr Cary told the inquest that he had attended the boy since he first became ill, and during that period up until his death Matthew had had fits of delirium in which he kept shouting out, 'Oh don't beat me, I will go to work'.[138] According to him, Matthew's feet were covered in chilblains, and because he was sent out in the snow they were very lacerated and had become gangrenous, which had been the cause of death.

The words of Robert Muirhead, another of Green's employees, were especially damning. He said that he had frequently seen his master beat Matthew with a heavy stick and with a strap with a buckle on it. It was no ordinary strap but the belly band of a horse. He went on to say that Green beat the boy seven or eight times a week and on the morning of 4 March he flogged him whilst he was in bed before sending him home to his mother in a cart.

According to the report in the *Southern Times*, the jury did not give much credence to Green's own evidence. He stated that he routinely sent his apprentices up chimneys to sweep them, but Matthew did the work so badly that he felt obliged to flog him.

In evidence, Dr Cary raised some doubt about the cause of death. He could not confirm that death resulted from ill treatment until a post-mortem had been carried out, but he thought that had proper treatment been obtained Matthew might have recovered. One thing that did not come out at the inquest was that Green had been employing Matthew illegally. Under the Chimney Sweeps Act of 1840, the minimum age of apprenticeship was 16.

---

138   *Southern Times* 19/3/1853.

In his summing up speech the coroner seemed to take a particularly light view of Green's behaviour. After telling the jury that in law the offence did not amount to manslaughter, he added that there was no doubt that the boy had been ill-treated by his master, 'who deserved to be severely reprimanded'.[139] The jury were clearly not impressed by the law and told the coroner that it was inadequate and that sixteen out of eighteen of them had agreed a verdict of manslaughter. Events took another turn then when the coroner decided to adjourn the inquest, pending the results of the post-mortem examination. One wonders why this was not carried out before the inquest. The jury gathered again the following Wednesday and heard from Dr Cary that the boy's death had been caused by a fever, no doubt exacerbated by ill-treatment and neglect. But he could not rule out that death might have been caused by the journey from Bridport to Lyme on the cart. Despite this the jury stuck to its guns and William Green was committed to Dorchester gaol to appear at the 1853 Lent assize.

When the presiding judge Mr Baron Martin charged the grand jury at the summer assizes he told them that he had directed that a separate bill be set up accusing Green of aggregated assault, based on the evidence of two doctors who concluded that the deceased died of chilblains. At the trial additional witnesses appeared, one confirming Matthew's good health when he was first employed, another the state of the injuries and another attesting to Green being a good man.

When the jury returned its verdict of guilty of common assault[140] the judge was not impressed, telling them that he felt they had been very lenient with the prisoner, and declared that, 'These poor boys had only the law to protect them, and persons must be taught that they must treat them in a proper manner'.[141] Given the verdict, Martin could only pass a sentence of eight months imprisonment, the prisoner having already served four. Green was also arraigned on the manslaughter verdict of the inquest jury, but no evidence was offered. It was not until 1875 that the chimney sweeping trade was licensed and properly regulated. Under that law sweeps had to be registered with the police and their work supervised.

***

---

139   Ibid.
140   Not so serious as aggravated assault, resulting in a lesser sentence.
141   *Salisbury Journal* 23/7/1853.

The scene at the opening of a case in the Crown Court on Wednesday 7 March 1866 was described by a reporter present in the court. 'The hearing of this case excited much excitement, the hall being crowded in every part, and, as the prisoners made their appearance in the dock, a general murmur seemed to run through the court.'[142] The prisoners referred to were Frederick Thomas Gumb, a tall, powerful-looking man, 30 years of age, who worked as a foreman at a silk factory in Sherborne, and his wife, Anna Maria Gumb, who in contrast was somewhat diminutive. Both were described as being 'respectably dressed, and appeared to be persons in a respectable position in life.'[143] The pair were charged with neglecting to supply their servant, Emily Fox, aged 14, with necessary food and also having caused her such bodily harm that endangered her life.

Like Matthew Leno, Emily Fox was a workhouse child. She was recommended by John Coran, the Master of the Union, to Mrs Gumb as a girl who would make a good servant, and it was agreed that she should be employed by them for a trial period of a month, but she would not be paid, just clothed and fed. Coran described Emily as a healthy, plump, good-looking girl. After the month had expired Anna Gumb said that she would take on the girl provided she was clothed, and clothing was duly supplied by the Board of Guardians. Emily started work for the Gumbs in May 1864, but six months later she left them and walked to the workhouse, but the staff would not let her in. Instead, they sent her back to her employers. It was Christmas Eve 1865 when Anna Gumb turned up at the workhouse with Emily, telling the Master that he must take the girl back because her husband would not let her sleep in the house any more. Coran told the court that he could hardly recognise her – that she was thin and dirty, her face was bruised and discoloured, and her 'nose was out of track', the latter observation comment producing some laughter in the court, despite the gravity of the case.

Dr William Williams was the medical officer for the Sherborne Union and attested that on Christmas Eve he was called to the infirmary where he found a young girl in one of the beds who appeared to be suffering from exhaustion. Examining her he found that she had no pulse, a remark that caused some commotion in the court, and her skin was cold like that of a dead body, but he could just detect a weak heartbeat. He declared that his first instinct was to turn away from her, thinking there was nothing that could be done to save her. But he changed his mind and had her body,

142   *Southern Times* 10/3/1866.
143   Ibid.

hands and feet rubbed and covered with blankets, and had a fire lit in the room. The bed was put in front of the fire and two women sat with her, feeding her gruel all night. The next night the doctor visited his patient and found her much revived and well enough to be examined properly. First, he weighed her and found that she tipped the scales at just 4 stone 4½ pounds (26.5 kg). He then examined her and found that she had a long scar across her forehead and a fresh bleeding wound on the lower part of her nose, and an old injury to her nose that had distorted it. This description provoked another reaction from the public gallery. A large area of Emily's back was covered with bruises and every joint and corner of a bone, such as the elbows and hips, had sores on them, typical of those a thin person would get lying on a hard bed. Overall, her body was extremely emasculated, and her legs were so thin that he could make his thumb and finger meet around the top of her thigh. This brought more gasps and murmuring from the court. The court was told that there was no evidence of any organic disease and that in the doctor's opinion her emaciated condition was caused by insufficient food, to a degree that her life was endangered. The blows to her body were, in his view, the result of external violence. On cross-examination the doctor admitted that he did not feel that Emily's health had been damaged permanently, but at the time he thought she was going to die.

It was Emily herself, 'a poor miserable looking girl',[144] who told how life was for her in the Gumb household. When she arrived she was given the job of nursing the Gumbs' two children and doing the housework. For her breakfast in the mornings she was given cold potatoes and cold cabbage and nothing else, which was repeated at lunchtime with the addition, two or three times a week, of a little meat. At 6.30 pm each day she was given bread and butter and sometimes dry bread to eat, but nothing more before she went to bed at about 11 pm. Emily explained that the cabbage and potatoes were cooked in one big batch at the beginning of the week and locked away in a safe. The safe she was referring to might have been a meat safe, but, either way, the audience in the court laughed at the idea. The Gumbs' diet was somewhat different. For breakfast they had fried potatoes and bacon, and eggs and bread and butter, and for lunch they had potatoes, meat and cabbage. As with Emily's food, anything left over was locked away. Frederick Gumb was obviously aware that Emily was being underfed because he told her to tell him when his wife did not give her enough to eat. Sometimes he

144   Ibid.

would give her bread and cheese, but only when his wife was out of the way. This induced more laughter from the court.

Emily made no accusations that her master hit her, but her mistress certainly did, on numerous occasions, with an ash sapling. One time she hit her across the bridge of the nose and broke it, and on another Emily was struck on the ear with a stick, making an open wound. Mrs Gumb decided to deal with the lesion herself by sewing up the ear with a needle and cotton, which Emily said was very painful. At this point Emily took off her hat in the court and showed the wound, which provoked expressions of sympathy. The list of hits, kicks and bruises continued, accompanied by gasps of amazement, until the young girl had finished her evidence.

Mr Karslake, who was representing Anna and Frederick Gumb, called just one witness, Robert Wilmott, who gave Frederick a good character reference. Karslake's main strategy was to question the credibility of Emily's version of events, for which he contended there was no corroboration. He asked the jury if they could believe that day after day, during the last three years she was in the service of Mr and Mrs Gumb, she was constantly being beaten and ill-treated by her mistress for no reasonable cause? And, if it was difficult to corroborate the evidence of the girl, it was impossible to confirm the alleged behaviour of his clients, given that all the assaults were committed in the family home, where the only witnesses were two children, too young to give evidence in court. He then turned his words on counsel for the prosecution, accusing him of exciting the sentiment of the court by saying that the defendants, after their ill-usage of the poor child, had 'left her like a dog to die in the workhouse hall'.[145]

This had been an emotionally charged case and Karslake must have suspected that there was very little chance of his clients being acquitted, given the appearance of the girl standing in the court and the evidence of the prosecution's witnesses. But there was one point of law that might just help them. Under the law as it was then, except under exceptional circumstances like murder or treason, a wife was not liable for crimes committed in the presence of her husband, as it was presumed she was acting under his coercion.[146]

In his comments to the jury Judge Byles told them that under statute it was Frederick Gumb who was responsible for ensuring his servant had the necessary food, clothing and lodging, and he saw no evidence that he had

---

145   Ibid.
146   Abolition of the presumption of coercion of a married woman by her husband was abolished by the Criminal Justice Act 1925.

wilfully neglected Emily; in fact he asked her to let him know if she was not being fed adequately. Neither was there any indication that any of the blows had been inflicted in his presence. But as the head of the household, on the other hand, it might be asked why he did not complain to his wife about her treatment of the child. In respect of Mrs Gumb, the judge said that they must consider whether, to her knowledge and with what power on her part, the food was improper and if she did bodily harm to her servant in the absence of her husband. It took the jury but a few moments of conferring to find the husband not guilty and the wife guilty. The sentence of twelve months imprisonment was received with applause.

***

One act of cruelty to a child that ended up in the Crown Court occurred on board a ship in Portland Roads.[147] Young lad John Williams, who was a racing jockey, lived in Rotherhithe in south-east London, an area long associated with shipping on the River Thames, where merchant vessels were constantly coming and going to unload and take on cargo at the Surrey Docks. It was there, in December 1857, that John met a Captain Metham, master of the merchant ship *Harriet*, who happened to be looking for someone to work in the ship's galley. John agreed and when the ship's cargo had been loaded they set off for France. On the return journey Metham headed for Portland in Dorset, arriving on a Thursday.

The next morning two customs house officers took the captain ashore, leaving John behind with another boy named Richard Pearce. They were left with orders to wash down the decks and cook some gruel for dinner. It was not until 10 pm that Metham returned, accompanied by Charles Norris, captain of the barque *Hollywood*, with some sailors and three boys. What happened next was told to the court by Richard Pearce. Metham and Norris came into the cabin where John was asleep on a bench and Richard was preparing some food. Metham went over to the bench and woke John up with a punch and then pulled him by his leg onto the floor. The two captains then sat down and drank some brandy and gin. After about an hour, Norris, looking over the fireplace, said, 'Hello, captain, you have a gun on board'. Metham then went to a locker, took out some flour, and after throwing it

---

147   A safe anchorage to the west of Portland, sheltered by Chesil Beach and the Isle of Portland.

at the young boy got some soot and rubbed it into his face. He then told Norris to take down the gun and give it to him, after which he took some gunpowder from a bag which normally contained shot, put some into the barrel of the gun and rammed it home. Giving the gun to Norris he told him to fire it at John, aiming just above or below the boy's body, but adding, 'there's no great sin in killing him'.[148]

The sound of the gun going off brought one of the sailors down to the cabin who, on seeing the lad's body on the floor, declared, 'Oh, he's gone – I do believe he's gone'.[149] Fortunately, John was not 'gone' and he was able to drag himself up from the floor. But he had received a flesh wound in the neck, caused by some shot that must have been mixed in with the powder. After eating some supper, and Norris having left, Metham reloaded the gun with powder and shot and aimed it at John. 'Don't fire – don't fire – there's shot in the gun; it will be sure to kill me',[150] he cried. Richard Pearce took the initiative and grabbed the gun and diverted the shot so that it hit the bulkhead. For some unaccountable reason Metham then took some scissors and cut off some of John's hair.

A couple of days later John went ashore, and some friends he was drinking with persuaded him to go to the police. As a result, the two men were arrested and committed to Dorchester prison. The case was heard in March 1858, and after hearing all the evidence, the jury found Metham and Norris guilty of unlawful wounding, but recommended leniency because they were both drunk. The judge expressed regret at having to pass sentence on the two men and ordered them to keep the peace for twelve months.

---

148 *Southern Times* 23/1/1858.
149 Ibid.
150 Ibid

A Very Violent Trade

Stories about smuggling in popular literature have a somewhat romantic air about them, whereas, in fact, it was a desperate and violent trade, where the perpetrators would go to extreme lengths not to get caught. All along the Dorset Coast gangs worked to bring in contraband from France and the Channel Islands. Goods were brought in by a boat which remained offshore until it was safe to land. Onshore, waiting for the smugglers, was someone who would signal, perhaps with a shout, whistle or light, that the coast was clear. Signalling to aid smugglers was an offence, but what exactly constituted a signal? This question was put to the test in the case of William White and a man named Jones.

White and Jones, both residents of the Isle of Portland, were indicted for raising a signal to a smuggling boat off the island in the early hours of 8 April 1826. The case for the prosecution in this instance rested on the evidence of two men of the preventative service who were stationed at Chesil Cove. The prisoners came unexpectedly across the two officers who were out on patrol, and when they saw the officers, they both whistled loudly. In the distance, through the darkness, the officers saw some men carrying tubs on their shoulders, who on hearing the alarm immediately jettisoned their cargo and ran towards the cliffs. At the same time a small boat near the shore put to sea. The men disbursed and about 15 tubs were recovered. Unfortunately for White and Jones, despite the darkness, the officers recognised them as persons who had previously been involved in smuggling and they were arrested.

Smuggling and poaching usually occurred in the hours of darkness when those out to catch them only had the light of lanterns to aid them.

Consequently, the defence often claimed mistaken identity. However, in this case Mr Williams representing the accused depended not on darkness for his defence but on the wording of a new clause that had been added to the Smuggling Act which stated that 'every intimation given to a smuggling boat or vessel, for the purpose of warning shall be deemed a signal'. Williams argued that even the most eminent philologist could not have thought of a word more vague than intimation. He contended that under the Act, if a man happened to be walking on Portland, and that a smuggling boat was nearby, and he whistled to his dog, or for that matter his grandma was with him and laughed loudly, neither of them could prove their innocence and could find themselves serving a year in gaol for a year. The new clause had

Giving the all clear to a smuggling boat. (Copyright, Illustrated London News/*Mary Evans Picture Library.)*

been criticised widely, but the Government explained that it was necessary because of the ingenuity with which those engaged in smuggling evaded the law. Another important point in the evidence was that the two officers did not agree on the time the whistling took place, one saying it was 1.30 and the other 2 o'clock.

The jury returned an innocent verdict, but the judge, Justice Gaselee, was not satisfied and asked the foreman if they believed the two men were together on the cliff. The foreman said yes but, overall, the evidence was not sufficient to convict either of the men. Gaselee then asked if they felt that the prisoners were there for warning smugglers. The foreman answered that as there was a variance in the time of the purported crime, they did not want to convict them. The prisoners were discharged.

***

A second case of smuggling was heard by the same court, but this time the charge was more serious. Isaac Rod was accused of maiming and dangerously wounding two officers, William Barnes and William Stephens. At about sunset on the evening of 10 January 1826 several men of the Portland coastguard preventative service, suspecting that contraband was about to be landed, searched about the neighbourhood of Church Hope [151]and came across a floating raft, from which they took 37 tubs of spirits. Suspecting there were more tubs to come ashore they hid among the rocks and soon spotted a boat a short distance out at sea creeping[152] for further booty. The officer in command told his men to do their duty, and on the boat coming into the shore Stephens seized one of the men named Richard Stone, and was endeavouring to secure him when another of the smugglers cried out, 'You shan't have him alive, we will have blood for blood'.[153] Stone broke away and gave a signal which resulted in about 30 or 40 men appearing, who pelted the officers unmercifully with stones, causing them to retreat for their lives. Several of them had wounds. Officer Stephens was ordered with some other men to go to the smuggling boat, *Prosperous*, and capture it. Whilst trying to take two of the smugglers off the boat he was hit on the side of the head by a large pebble, which knocked him into the sea. While he lay insensible in the shallow water, another man, believed to be the prisoner Rod, came up to him and deliberately threw a stone at his head, which fractured his skull. On seeing what had happened, officer Barnes cried out, 'Oh my God, you have done murder'.[154] Barnes was then attacked by several of the smugglers, beaten severely and had his jaw dislocated. It seemed as if the Government men were losing the battle, but fortunately for them reinforcements arrived, and the smugglers were eventually driven off. Stephens survived the vicious attack, but it was nearly three weeks before he could leave his home and help in the arrest of Rod, although he was uncertain of his identity.

One interesting feature of smuggling cases it that they usually produced no end of witnesses for the defence willing to tell the court of the good character of the accused. In this case, several described the prisoner Rod as industrious, upright, sober and a good-natured young man. Despite this, he was found guilty and it was time for Justice Gaselee to pass sentence. A recent Act of Parliament had made it a capital offence to wound or use any weapon

---

151   Also known as Church Ope.
152   Retrieving tubs from the water. Tubs containing contraband were covered in tar and then sunk beneath a boat to be pulled up when the craft was inshore.
153   *Chronicle* 16/3/1826.
154   Ibid.

against any officer or others employed in the prevention of smuggling, so he had little option but to pronounce the death sentence. However, given the fact that this was the first case since the new Act, plus the testimonies of the character witnesses supporting the prisoner, he did hold out a slight hope that Rod's life would be spared.[155] On 29 April the convicted man received a royal pardon from King George IV, on the condition that he serve two years imprisonment with hard labour.

***

Sometimes battles between Government officers and smugglers had fatal consequences, as was the outcome of a crime committed near West Lulworth, after which two men appeared before Justice Patteson at the summer assizes of 1832. The *Salisbury Journal* remarked that the case excited great interest.[156]

Scratchers' Bottom[157] is a clifftop valley situated on the Purbeck coast between Durdle Door and Swyre Head. The landward end and the sides of the valley are farmland and at the seaward end cliffs tower 100 ft above the waves. At about 10 pm on 28 June, on a clear starlit night, a boat was being rowed toward the small cove at the bottom of the cliffs. It was spotted by Thomas Brewer, an officer in the newly formed coastguard service, who was out on duty on the cliffs, walking towards Durdle Door. Keeping out of sight he went down to the shore where he found four men there and the boat gone. He told the court that he took notice of them and noted that one of them, who he identified as the prisoner James Davis, was wearing a long frock coat and a hat that had been painted black, perhaps as camouflage in the darkness. He approached them and asked what business they had there at that time of night, to which they replied that they had come from Weymouth for pleasure. He told them they had come a long way from the east and not from the west, the direction of Weymouth, which they denied. There then followed some verbal abuse from the men before they went on up the cliff. Not satisfied, the officer went to where the boat had been and gone and found 29 tubs of spirit lying on the beach, containing 88 gallons of white brandy. The tubs had been tied together to make them easier to carry. Brewer realised that he would need some help removing the contraband, so

---

155   National Archives HO13 Home Office: correspondence and warrants.
156   *Salisbury Journal* 6/8/1832.
157   Known now as Scratchy Bottom.

he burned a blue light and fired several shots into the air, the usual signal that would summon men from the coastguard station at nearby Kimmeridge. It was not long before James Lifton and brothers Ralph and Thomas Teed came to his assistance. Brewer may have thought that was that, the smugglers had gone and he merely had to get the tubs to the customs house in Weymouth. But, just as help arrived, he looked up at the top of the cliff where he saw at least 50 people assembled. The officers ran towards the bottom of the cliff to prevent the mob from coming down to rescue the tubs and Lifton called up, demanding to know why they were there. He told them that the officers had seized the goods and they would not have them, to which the crowd assured him that they would and started firing guns. The gunfire was returned, and the skirmish went on for about three-quarters of an hour, after which the crowd suddenly left. It was then that cries of someone moaning could be heard from the top of the cliff.

The cliff at Scratcher's Bottom, today called Scratchy Bottom, over which Lt. Knight was thrown. (Author copyright.)

While the gun battle was taking place another more sinister drama was unfolding up on the cliff. Among those that set out from the Kimmeridge coastguard station to help Brewer was a Lieutenant Knight, who along with John Duke made their way along the cliff path towards Scratchers' Bottom. Arriving there they saw a large group of men each carrying a stick about 7 ft long and heard some of them firing pistols. As the officers were going down the hill to help their colleagues on the beach, they were attacked by about a dozen of the men, whom they told that if they used their sticks they would receive the contents of their pistols. The attackers, disregarding the threat, began using their sticks, which the officers warded off with their cutlasses. Other assailants joined in and formed a circle around the two men, who were now standing back to back. Knight fired a shot over the heads of the crowd and then into them, fearing for his life, but the two men were overwhelmed and eventually knocked to the ground, where the beating continued. As John Duke was being dragged down the path, continuously being attacked, he heard Knight say, 'What brutes they are!' Then he heard from somewhere in the crowd someone say, 'Let us throw the _____ [sic] over the cliff'.[158] A man then interfered and prevented Duke being thrown over the cliff. By now he had received several wounds and one of the men had broken his stick on his arm, leading to one of the gang saying to the others, 'He bleeds well and breathes short; it will soon be over with him'.[159] Leaving him for dead the attackers disbursed and Duke managed to climb up the cliff path where he saw Knight's petticoat trousers,[160] and when afterwards he went down to the beach he found Knight lying close to the cliff, moaning, unable to speak and insensible. He had obviously been thrown over the cliff. The injured man was taken to Lulworth, where he died the next day. A reward of £1,000 was offered for information leading to the arrest of any of the smugglers.

James Davis and Charles Bascombe were the two men in the dock facing a charge not relating to the death of Lt Knight but of 'feloniously assembling, with other persons unknown, armed with fire-arms and other offensive weapons, in order to aid and assist in the running and carrying away prohibited goods, which are liable to pay certain duties to the customs'.[161] John Duke was the principal witness for the prosecution who attested that Davis and Bascombe were among the men who encircled him and it was Bascombe who hit him with a stick. He had not known the man previously but he did know Davis.

The defence's case was simply that neither of the men was there on the night in question. For Bascombe, four witnesses claimed that he was in bed by 10 o'clock that night and did not leave his house until 4 the next morning, when he went to thatch a rick of clover. For Davis, five witnesses swore that he was at home all that night, and in bed early next morning because he had a sore foot.

---

158 *Salisbury Journal* 6/8/1832.
159 Ibid.
160 Trousers with very baggy legs.
161 *Salisbury Journal* 6/8/1832.

In his summing up Justice Patteson told the jury that in coming to their decision they should consider the fact that although Duke knew the person and the name of Davis, he did not mention it at the inquest into Knight's death, or until the last day of the magistrates' inquiry. This, he felt, was suspicious. After ten minutes' deliberation the prisoners were found not guilty. The killers of Lt Knight were never brought to justice.

***

The typical picture of a confrontation between the Revenue and those importing illegal goods is of men unloading casks from a boat and being challenged by Government officials, but the work of the Revenue men did not stop there. They also had the job of checking that spirits were legal wherever they were being sold.

On 16 September 1829 Weymouth races were being held, and among the crowd were three excise officers named May, Hutchings and Hall. They were there to visit all the booths selling liquors, to ascertain whether duty had been paid on them. Towards the end of the day Hall and May visited the last booth whilst Hutchings held May's horse outside. He had just mounted it when some men came up to him and asked him to leave immediately, using bad language. One of them asked him if there was any harm in killing a toad, which he ignored. The question was asked several times in an intimidatory way, so to placate them he said he thought there was no harm and was answered that there was no more harm in killing an excise man. Trying to avoid a confrontation, Hutchings tried to ride off but was jostled by the mob, which rapidly increased in number and many tried to pull him from his horse. Inside the booth May and Hall heard the commotion and came out, a signal for the crowd to leave Hutchings and rush toward them. As the mob approached, using threatening language, May, who had with him two pistols, one loaded and one not, pulled out the unloaded one and presented it to the crowd, ordering them to keep back. Instead, they rushed at him and wrestled the firearm out of his hand. Enter onto the scene constable Tantrum, to bring order, who for his efforts was struck on the head by a man named Squibb and then kicked. Hutchings made his escape followed by a shower of stones and a chasing group of attackers.

The men in the dock were Joseph Squibb and Henry Beale, whose representatives tried to prove through cross-examination that the officers were intoxicated. The two were found guilty and told that they would be discharged on their own recognizances[162] for good behaviour and be brought up for sentencing if they misbehaved.

***

Chesil Beach is a natural bank of pebbles and shingle which runs for 29 km from West Bay near Bridport to the Isle of Portland. Behind the bank is a tidal lagoon, known as the Fleet, which made the area an ideal place for smugglers. After tubs had been landed at the seashore they could be sunk in the lagoon, where they could be retrieved at a later date.

This photograph shows the Fleet lagoon and Chesil Beach at Abbotsbury. The Fleet was an ideal place for smugglers to hide their contraband, to be retrieved later. (Author copyright.)

In the early morning of Thursday 11 September 1834, a small boat was making its way towards the beach at Abbotsbury. In it were a local gang of smugglers and a quantity of contraband. At the same time as the boat was approaching the shore, John Wood, a coastguard officer, happened to be in

---

162 A bond by which a person undertakes before a court or a magistrate to observe some condition, especially to appear when summoned to a court, usual under a penalty of a fine on default.

the vicinity when he heard a whistle from behind him. Suspecting that some smuggling was going on, he shouted to the men in the boat to 'Come along', meaning for them to land near him. All of a sudden he saw a large party of men coming onto the beach, he thought about 60 or 70, most of whom were carrying large sticks or bludgeons and some were carrying swingles;[163] the group came toward him, beating their sticks on the stones, and someone shouted, 'Murder the _____!' [sic]. As the mob came closer Wood realised that discretion was the better part of valour and ran along the beach, to cries of 'Catch the _____' [sic] coming from behind him. Fortunately, he ran into another officer, Robert Cox, and the two of them confronted the crowd, Cox firing a gun over their heads. This provoked someone throwing a stone at his chest, followed by someone knocking him down with a stick, seizing his musket and ammunition, and tying his hands together. By now

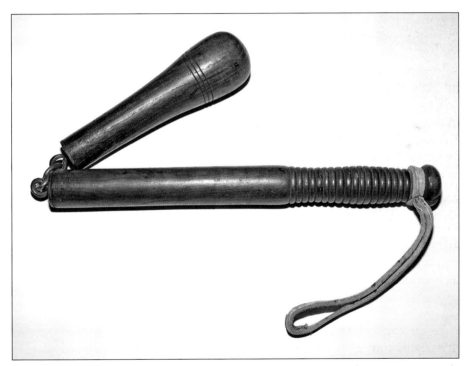

Based on a larger version used for corn threshing, the swingle was a favourite weapon of the smuggler. It was very effective and easily concealed. (Courtesy of Shire Hall Historic Courthouse Museum.)

163   The swingle was a favourite weapon of smugglers. It consisted of two heavy pieces of wood joined by a chain (see photo).

more coastguard officers had arrived and a battle ensued. Lt Rowe, who was among them, recognised one of the smugglers as William Whittle, who was in his shirt sleeves and wearing a southwester. Rowe made a beeline for Whittle and attempted to arrest him, but he was felled by a blow from him with the bludgeon he carried. Whittle was eventually arrested, as were three others – John Crewe, John Hall and Henry Seal.

The four men stood in the court at the 1835 Lent assizes, charged with assembling with bludgeons for the purpose of carrying and running prohibited goods, and as far as the law was concerned each man was equally culpable if found guilty, even though Whittle was the only one to have used violence. Under an Act of Parliament, if three or more men assembled together armed with offensive weapons for the purpose of landing prohibited goods, they were guilty of a felony. Whittle, in his defence, said that he would not have attacked Lt Rowe if he had known him, and brought two witnesses, including the local vicar, to speak of his good character. The reverend gentleman told the jury that Whittle had served an apprenticeship for four years as a sailor and had always conducted himself well. A person named West, who had employed Crewe, said he had always found him hard-working and industrious. The brother of Seal, in whose house at Puncknowle the prisoner lodged, assured the court that the prisoner had gone to bed that night between 9 and 10 o'clock and did not leave the house until 5 the next morning. Counsel for the defence had contested the use of the word bludgeon, as opposed to the word stick, as it gave the impression of a weapon of violence. But the judge, holding one up before the court, said that there could be no doubt that it was a bludgeon.

Seal was acquitted, because of the lack of positive identification in the darkness, but the other three men were found guilty. Before recording a verdict of death Baron Gurney addressed the prisoners, saying how lamentable it was to see them in such a situation, especially Whittle, who had been respectable. He added that he would recommend to His Majesty to spare their lives. True to his word, an appeal was made to the Home Secretary, and the sentences of the three convicted men were commuted from the death penalty The decision on Crewe and Hall's appeal, dated 1 May 1835, was sent to the Earl of Ilchester, at Melbury House, near Sherborne and read: 'In the absence of Lord John Russell I am directed to acquaint yourself, that the sentence of death, recorded against John Crewe and John Hall at the last Dorset assizes for assembling with others armed for the purposes of landing foreign spirits in whose behalf yourself have interested yourself has recently been commuted to one year's imprisonment on the recommendation of the judge before whom they were tried.' Whittle's sentence was reduced to transportation for ten years.

Whittle embarked on the prison ship *Royal Sovereign* in July 1835, landing in New South Wales on 12 December. He spent the rest of his life in Australia and in 1874 he died, aged 63 years.

Record of Crewe and Hall's commuted sentence recommended by Baron Gurney. (Crown copyright.)

***

The smuggling trade to a large extent was the natural result of government policies. Successive governments imposed more punitive customs and excise duties on imported things like wine, brandy and tea, to help fund successive wars, making the illegal importation of goods very profitable. Things changed in the 1840s when free trade was introduced and import taxes were reduced. This signalled the end of what might be termed the golden age of smuggling and within 10 years large-scale smuggling had disappeared.

Two Cases of Great Gravity

When giving his charge to the grand jury at the summer assizes of 1869, judge Sir Robert Lush said that though the number of cases to be heard were few, two of them were of great gravity. He was referring to two murders, both of which would provoke comment after the trials, one because of the behaviour of the accused and the other for its controversial verdict.

The first case concerned Jonah Detheridge, a 25-year-old career criminal who was serving a seven-year prison sentence with hard labour at Portland prison. He had been sent there following a conviction at Stafford assizes in January 1865. The crime for which he was charged with was stealing a purse containing one shilling and eleven-pence, for which he was sent first to Stafford gaol, where his conduct was described as good. After a probationary period of six months he was transferred to Pentonville prison, where his behaviour was markedly different. He became belligerent and uncooperative, a manner that went with him when he was transferred to Portland to serve out his sentence.

Portland prison was opened in 1848, for prisoners who had been sentenced to hard labour. The demand for stone from Portland's quarries provided extremely hard work for the convicts. In 1862 the Government started to build six gun batteries at East Weare to protect Portland harbour. On 26 March 1869 a group of 25 convicts were working on Battery No.1,[164] supervised by assistant prison warder Joseph Trevitt, assisted by another warder named James Holmes. Trevitt was standing on an embankment about 8 ft high, overlooking the men at work. Detheridge was one of the group and he been given the job of dressing the blocks of stone which would form the outside of the casement. The warder was not happy about Detheridge's work and told him to be more careful, to which the prisoner said that he would do the work in his own way. This led to further words. Trevitt said that he would not be spoken to like that, provoking a response that the prisoner would speak to him as he liked. Saying no more, the warder walked away. This happened at about 10 am and what happened an hour later was described in the court.

Giving evidence, Henry Davis, a convict who was part of the working party, said that he was about to pick up his wheelbarrow when he saw one of the convicts leave his place and go up a plank. The man was Detheridge,

---

164   Some reports say it was Battery No. 4.

Convicts working in one of Portland's quarries. (Courtesy of Portland Museum.)

who then approached Trevitt from behind, raised his stone axe and planted the pointed end into the man's skull. Trevitt fell sideways down the embankment, followed by Detheridge who gave one more savage blow to Trevitt's head and another to the neck. He then ran off, followed by the witness and warder Holmes. Robert Pearce, an assistant warder, heard a cry of 'Stop him,' looked round and saw Holmes chasing the prisoner, sword in hand. He managed to catch Detheridge and put him back into his cell. What happened next was recorded by the Governor of the prison in his record book: '4935 J Detheridge was searched in the presence of the police and Major Hickey the Chief Warder. Handed over into the charge of Superintendent Underwood for removal to Dorchester gaol to await his trial for the murder of assistant warder Trevitt. His conduct at noon was outrageous, he yelled and made use of murderous language towards myself and the officers personally.' Although this behaviour continued in the run-up to his trial, unlike Edwin Preedy[165] this prisoner maintained an indifferent and superior attitude throughout his trial, sometimes staring at any witness who said anything he did not like.

In the courtroom Elgar Blacker, the medical officer, described Trevitt's injuries and said that he had tried to staunch the bleeding. It was Blacker who did the post-mortem on the body, which he stated had been struck with great force and sustained terrible wounds. These gruesome details caused one woman in the public gallery to faint, provoking Detheridge to ask the judge who she was, repeating the request several times. Asked if he had anything to say in his defence, Detheridge said that he wanted the Governor to describe his behaviour to the court. The Governor said it was very bad. He was a man of ungovernable temper who, however, at times had been very good. He had made murderous threats to the staff and been punished on several occasions for misdemeanours. With no barrister to represent him, that was the beginning and end of Detheridge's defence and the jury immediately found him guilty. He appeared to be unconcerned about the verdict and even smiled when Justice Lush put on the black cap and pronounced a death sentence. His last words before leaving the court were, 'I shall not be the first innocent man hung'.[166]

The date set for the execution was 12 August, over three weeks from the date of the trial, giving Detheridge plenty of time to confess his sins and seek forgiveness from God, under the guidance of Rev. L.B. Watson, chaplain of the prison. But he would have none of it and refused any advice or solace. On the night before the fateful day the condemned man slept well, to the extent that the warders had to wake him up and then he ate a good breakfast.

It had been six years since the last hangings in Dorchester, those of Edwin Preedy and Charles Fooks,[167] and they had been the last public executions in the town. Now all hangings had to take place inside the prison grounds away from the eyes of the public. Unfortunately, the usual attendees at Dorchester's hangings had not heard the news and quite a crowd made their way to the county town, only to be disappointed. On this occasion the scaffold was erected in Trial Ward No.2, completely shut away from public view. The only spectators were Mr J. Lawrence, the prison governor, his deputy, the Under-Sheriff, a few warders and representatives of the press. According to reporters present, Detheridge looked sullenly at Calcraft, the executioner, but showed

---

165　See page 150.
166　*The Scotsman* 13/8/1869.
167　See page 155.

no fear and when he reached the scaffold he tried to run up the steps but tripped. Accompanying Detheridge to the scaffold was Rev. Mann, who took him by the hand and in an earnest tone said, 'Try to pray, pray to your Lord to have mercy on you', to which the reply was, 'Who must I pray to? Who has brought me here? That is what I want to know. Has God brought me here?' Mann responded, 'I want you to try to be saved. The Lord have mercy on you.' Mann then shook hands with him and said, 'Goodbye, God bless you'. Detheridge's last words as Calcraft put the hood over his head were, 'Pray to the Lord to save me' and 'What are these men here for?'[168] Under a new law it was required to hold a post-mortem after a hanging, in front of a jury, before the burial. But, before Detheridge's body was taken for interment inside the prison walls there was one more procedure to be carried out. Dr Good, the prison surgeon, who was researching the physiognomy of criminals to see if there was a criminal type, had a plaster cast made of the dead man's head. Many such masks were made are popularly referred to as death masks.

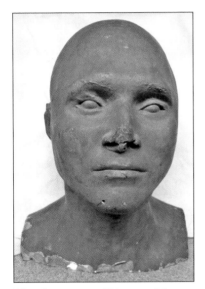

The plaster cast of 23-year-old Jonah Detheridge. Physically, he was described as a short man, 5 ft 7 in tall, stocky, thick set, pock-marked, and with a low forehead. (Courtesy of Dorset Museum.)

Jonah Detheridge's trial and subsequent execution were published nationally by the newspapers and it was not long before some of them used the occasion to slip into literary overdrive. Two days after the trial an article appeared in the *Daily Telegraph*. It opened by suggesting that Detheridge's body might inspire the same feelings invoked by that of a dead tiger, describing them both as 'two bodies formerly full of hate and murder, now lifeless, made so in Detheridge's case by Calcraft's craft'. It then turned to the prisoner's behaviour on the gallows, saying, 'There are those who conquer the fear of death by religious faith, by philosophy, by the consciousness of a good life, by the frenzy of battle or the sweet passion of self-sacrifice; but this man Detheridge with no such aids or incentives went his way to the other world gay with despair, and calm with the courage of an indomitable ferocity.' The article suggested

168   *Daily Telegraph* 14/8/1869.

Funeral procession of assistant warder Joseph Trevitt, passing through Easton, on its way to St George's Reforne church. (Courtesy of the Grove Prison Museum.)

that should he have been taken from his cradle as a baby and brought up in a respectable home this courage and fortitude may have 'made him a hero, a great soldier, a resistless admiral, a conqueror without fear or failure'. Finally it asked, 'Is there anything in the infinite forces of the world as wonderful as that we call the soul of man, sometimes beautiful, sometimes, as here, terrible?'[169]

***

The other murder trial heard at the same assize was just as terrible but the victim was very different. Cases of infanticide were tragic for all concerned and when they came before the court in Dorset the judges were careful to advise the grand jury on what constituted murder and what comprised concealment of birth. When the case of the death of a child near Wimborne came to court and the evidence had been heard, there could not have been much doubt in the opinion of the majority in attendance which category it came under. In the nineteenth century the crime of infanticide was associated with that class of society the establishment referred to as the 'lower orders'. Typically, a woman who fell pregnant with an illegitimate child was in service in a household, worked on the land or was a factory girl. It was not a crime that was associated with the middle and upper classes; but there were exceptions.

---

169   Ibid.

On Tuesday 15 June 1869 an inquest was held at the Cricketers Arms public house, Wimborne. The jury, which consisted of local tradesmen and farmers, were about to hear the harrowing facts surrounding the death of a newly born baby boy. The coroner, Mr Rawlings, would have been aware that some of the jury may well have known a young lady by the name of Emma Pitt or members of her family and, if not, they would certainly have heard rumours of the horror that had occurred at a local school. He therefore felt bound to remind them that even though this was a most distressing case they were 'bound to deal with it openly, fairly, and in an open manner, as before God, and to return a verdict according to the evidence, and nothing more'.[170]

John Pitt was a respected cordwainer[171] who lived in Wimborne High Street. Two of his children were equally respected, especially in their careers. His eldest son John had the important job of District Relieving Officer,[172] whilst his youngest daughter Emma had trained as a teacher and worked at the National School at Park Homer, Hampreston. It was in May of 1869 that someone took Emma aside and told her that local gossips were saying that she was pregnant, something the 24-year-old unmarried girl refuted indignantly.

Witness Elizabeth Parsons, who lived near the school where Emma worked, explained what happened a few weeks later. One day Julia Guy, a pupil teacher, arrived at her house and asked her to go to the school where one of the teachers was ill. In consequence of what the young lady told her she went immediately and on arrival proceeded upstairs. Emma still lived with her parents but had a room above the school, and it was there that Mrs Parsons found her kneeling on the floor, with her head and hands on the bed. Mrs Parsons asked if she were ill, to which the kneeling girl replied that she was very ill and had been so since 3 o'clock in the morning. Emma then asked if she could get her a little ginger to help with the wind she had in her stomach. Returning home, Mrs Parsons found some ginger and gave it to Julia Guy to take back to the school. Concerned about what she had seen, Mrs Parsons decided to go back to the school, where she found Emma downstairs in great pain, but after taking some brandy she said she felt better and would go upstairs to rest. Again, Mrs Parsons went back home, but after a short while two schoolgirls knocked on her door, asking her to take a cup of tea to their schoolmistress. This time, when she went

---

170   *Western Gazette* 25/6/1869.
171   A maker of shoes, as opposed to a cobbler who mended shoes.
172   The job of District Relieving Officer was to administer the poor law in his area.

into Emma's room she found her lying on the bed and thought she looked very ill and could barely sit up to drink the tea. Once again, Mrs Parsons returned home, doubtlessly thinking that she would keep an eye on Emma. However, a little later Julia Guy appeared at her door again, asking her not to go to see Miss Pitt anymore as she was feeling better and was going home. Given the condition Emma was in just an hour ago, Mrs Parsons found this odd and went back to the school yet again. When she got there, she found that the front door had been bolted from the inside, so she went round the back and found another door open. It was when she was just inside that she heard a loud knock coming from upstairs, which sounded like something falling on the floor. Shouting up the stairs, she asked if she could help and Emma requested more tea and after drinking it said that she felt much better and intended to walk home. Clearly, she was in no condition to do that, so despite the schoolmistress's objections it was agreed that Mrs Parsons' son would drive her home to her parents in his cart. It was when Emma was being helped up into the cart that Mrs Parsons noticed blood on her dress. She now suspected that the rumours were true and a confinement had taken place, so went upstairs to investigate, where she found the room saturated with blood. Clearly, a birth had happened, but where was the baby? By this time other women had turned up at the school, including Emma's sister and a Mrs Birch, and it was the latter who found the body of a newly born male child under a piece of patchwork in the top drawer of a chest of drawers. She was horrified by what she discovered. Blood was running from the corner of the baby's mouth and the other corner was cut, and there were injuries to the head. On the floor was a large stone with blood on it.

Superintendent Hammond attended the scene and after questioning those present ordered PC Adams to take the body of the child to Wimborne police station. Adams deposed that when he went to collect the body he looked in the child's mouth and found that the tongue was missing. It was found in the corner of the drawer wrapped in a piece of cloth, tied with ribbon. Last to give evidence was Wimborne surgeon Dr William Druitt, who after describing the extensive injuries declared that in his view the child had been born alive. The evidence concluded it was now time for the jury to consider its verdict, which it did and came back with a judgement of wilful murder by the mother.

Newspaper reports of the inquest ensured that on the day of Emma's trial in Dorchester the public gallery was full and the first thing Judge Lush did was to order all the women and children to leave because of the horrific details of the medical evidence. When Emma was brought up from the cells the reporters present noted that she had a youthful look, was of slight build and appeared very weak. Given this, she was allowed to be seated throughout the proceedings. When asked how she pleaded to the charge of wilful murder of her male child she quietly replied, 'Not guilty'. The witnesses who were present at the inquest gave their stories once again and Dr Druitt went into more detail about the injuries on the body. His conclusion was that they could not have occurred during childbirth but had been inflicted afterwards. It took the jury just ten minutes to make up its mind but the verdict was not what most people in the court thought it would be. Emma was found not guilty of murder but guilty of concealment of a birth. Hope must have risen in Emma's heart because punishments for concealment were normally

The assize court was a daunting place for a woman accused of infanticide or concealment. She faced a male judge, male lawyers, an all-male jury and often a hostile public gallery. (Courtesy of the British Library.)

light, perhaps a few months or even weeks in prison. But Judge Lush was obviously not impressed by the jury's verdict and sentenced her to two years imprisonment with hard labour. Emma was led from the court room crying and sighing.

As with the case of Louisa Walborn,[173] the jury's decision led to extensive coverage in the press. Reports circulating around Wimborne were that the father of Emma's child was a married man, which may have been one reason why she acted so desperately. Of course, there was no mention or enquiry made about the father at the trial; there rarely was in such cases – something that was noted by some newspapers. The *Morning Advertiser* saw no reason why Emma Pitt should not have been found guilty, but it did understand why the jury was not prepared to condemn her to the sacrifice of her life. It argued that there was a widespread and just feeling that if full justice were to be done to the mother then the father of the murdered child ought to be made to stand in the dock beside the mother, and until this happened juries would recognise the inequality against the mother and not visit the full use of the law upon her.[174] *The Atlas* newspaper was very emphatic on the reasons why such a terrible crime existed. It told its readers:

'If there be anything in our courts of justice to stir with deep emotion the hearts of English jurymen, to unman the sternest of our English judges and to make even counsel for the prosecution slacken in their efforts to procure their efforts to procure the conviction of the accused, it is when one of these poor creatures stands trembling and weeping at the bar. One knows so well the history of events which have led to the commission of the great crime. It is the same always, only with local and accidental variations, or such slight changes as may result from temperament or education. There has been temptation, difficult to resist, when there is a fond woman's heart, with all its weaknesses, to be beguiled – there has been opportunity aiding temptation – there has been innocence and blind confidence, and fullest truth on the one side; on the other fraud, treachery, hard heartedness, or slavish fear. She has awakened from the dream of love to find herself ruined, deserted, disgraced, almost before she had given one serious thought to the perilous downward path that she was treading:

"The road is dim, the current unperceived,
The weakness painful and most pitiful,
By which a virtuous woman, in pure youth,
May be delivered to stress and shame."

---

173   See page 140.
174   *Morning Advertiser* 30/7/1869.

'And so, often it is that virtuous women, in the very purity of their youth, are delivered to distress and shame; and the burden of their shame is so grievous, that when the hour of trial comes upon them they seek to escape from it, by laying, in their anguish and desperation – often, indeed, in their insanity – violent hands on the helpless creature, born to them to be a life's reproach. They scarcely know what they are doing until the law has laid its relentless hand upon them; and then they learn how they have plunged into a lower abyss of wickedness and shame. The causes of this are very obvious. In the first place, there is the heartlessness of the companion of the poor girl's guilt. No woman destroys her illegitimate offspring, unless she has been deserted by her betrayer, or he aids and abets her in the commission of the crime. In either case he is morally and accessory to its commission. Yet, trial after trial takes place (unhappily these trials are becoming more and more frequent), and the name of the father of the murdered child is not even brought before the public. If the great aim of the law be to prevent, rather than to punish crime, no more effective mode of accomplishing this great end could be devised than that of threating the father of the child as an accessory. The other great incentive to child murder, in these cases, is an overwhelming sense of the injury which is inflicted on the worldly prospects of the mother, by the revelation of her maternity. "I am ruined. I am about to become an outcast. I see nothing before me but beggary and prostitution. Can I not obviate this by concealment?" A slight pressure of the fingers will destroy the little life of the child of shame. Thus the crime is committed. But if we were a little more just, a little more tolerant, a little more discriminating, all this, perhaps, might not happen. We turn our backs somewhat too hastily upon those who have stooped to folly, and forget that perhaps they are not weaker or more criminal than their neighbours.'[175]

---

175   *The Atlas* 31/7/1869.

The Not So Faithful Servants

On 16 March 1823 brothers Thomas and William Harvey and their uncle Thomas Dossiter stood in the small dock in Dorchester assize court watching Judge Baron Hullock don the black cap signifying that they had been sentenced to death for a robbery – William Harvey and Thomas Dossiter for perpetrating the crime and Thomas Harvey for being an accessory before the fact.

Dossiter was born in 1778 in the small village of Elstow in Bedfordshire. He followed his father's trade as a baker and at the age of 17 he went to London, where, according to the *Salisbury Journal*, he 'became idle and dissipated and falling into bad company, quitted the paths of honesty'.[176] On one occasion he was convicted of theft and received a sentence of transportation, but served his time in a prison hulk where he met another prisoner by the name of Robert Whales, alias Smith, a man who would also play a part in this story.

Also born at Elstow were brothers 24-year-old Thomas and 31-year-old William Harvey. Their father, who was a dealer in pigs, died when they were young, and both went into service. Thomas from the age of 11 worked in several places as a groom. William, after being apprenticed to a baker, joined the household of Lady Caroline Damer, who lived at Milton Abbey, Milton Abbas, and had worked for her for 16 years up to the time of his arrest.

On the night of Tuesday 14 January 1823 William Harvey and Thomas Dossiter climbed a high wall surrounding the outer courtyard of Milton Abbey and then knocked a hole in the wall of the house sufficient to allow Harvey to get through. Once inside the house he unbolted the main door of the building and let his accomplice in. Reporting on the break-in, the *Chester Courant* commented that, 'There is no doubt entertained, from the manner in which the robbery was affected, that the perpetrators were well acquainted with the premises'.[177] Once inside the building the pair made for the strong room and managed somehow to break their way into it, no easy task as it was of solid iron and secured by two iron bars. Inside the men found their booty, upwards of a ton of gold and silver plate, including a complete table service of gold dishes, covers, plates, knives and forks. Most of it they dumped into the nearby pond, presumably with the intention of coming back to retrieve it at a later date. They carried off about half the silver, reckoned to be worth

---

176   *Salisbury Journal* 7/4/1823.
177   *Chester Courant* 14/1/1823.

about £16,000, over one million pounds in today's value. Considering the noise they must have made and the duration of the robbery it is remarkable that the servants heard nothing.

The robbery was discovered the next morning when some boys found a few knives and forks scattered around the lake, and when it was dredged the majority of the haul was found. The hunt was on for the perpetrators of the crime and it was not long before the police were also looking for Thomas Harvey, who was eventually caught at Buriton in Hampshire in the house of his wife's father.

At the trial, after the prosecution had made its case, it was time for the defendants to defend themselves. What followed was an altercation at the bar between Thomas Dossiter and Thomas Harvey, each blaming the other for masterminding the robbery. Whales, also a member of the gang, had already turned King's evidence and incriminated the others. Dossiter declared that the Harvey brothers were always on at him to get him to assist in robbing their mistress's house. He declared that he did not like the sound of the job but eventually agreed to do it. He contended that on 27 December William visited him and said that the work had to be done quickly, as Mr Evans, Lady Caroline's Steward, had just left to join her in London. On their way to the break-in Thomas Harvey and Thomas Dossiter stopped off for some beer and discussed the job, Harvey saying that he would be happy with £400, the other that he would be happy with a good deal less. Dossiter told the court that Harvey would try to persuade them that it was Dossiter who entered the building first but in fact it was Harvey.

At this point Thomas Harvey interrupted the proceedings saying that it was all lies and malice and, facing Dossiter, he accused him of planning the whole thing, saying that he and Whales were the life and soul of it, and pointing out that they were both previous offenders. William Harvey declined to say anything in his defence.

After a lengthy summing up by the judge the jury retired for just a few minutes before bringing in a guilty verdict. According to a reporter in the court there was then a solemn pause before the judge began to announce the sentence in a faltering voice. He was obviously much affected by the case of the three men and addressed them directly, saying, 'You have been convicted of a crime of the deepest dye, after a patient hearing, and I wish for your sakes that I could entertain the slightest doubt in your favour, or see a circumstance in mitigation of the crime. But your case, William Harvey, is attended by circumstances of peculiar enormity. That you, who have lived for sixteen years in the service of an excellent mistress, should suggest and engage in such a robbery; that you, in whom a trust was reposed, should betray it in such a foul manner.'[178] After the judge had completed the sentence in barely a whisper William Harvey collapsed in the dock and was carried off, unconscious, with the other prisoners to the county gaol, to await their execution.

The time set for the hanging was 3 pm on Saturday 5 April at the new drop in front of Dorchester prison. They had almost three weeks to contemplate their fate, repent their sins and make their peace with God. The three were immediately penitent of what they had done. On the Sunday after the trial, at the request of Thomas Harvey, Robert Wales, the man who had turned King's evidence, was granted an interview with the prisoners. The Harveys begged for his forgiveness for involving him in the crime and entreated him to lead a better life. Thomas Harvey and Thomas Dossiter, who had entered the gaol as enemies after accusing each other in the court, were now meeting regularly in the prison and could be seen in prayer together. On the Wednesday before the execution the men were given the opportunity to say goodbye to their loved ones. The *Salisbury Journal* reported that the scene was one that was more easily imagined than described, and that the supressed screams of the women and the sobs of the men were truly heart-rending.[179] For the prisoners and their families it was a terrible time, exacerbated by the fact that a few days earlier several newspapers had reported erroneously that the men had been granted a reprieve.

While the three were in prison they related a curious phenomenon. They said that on their return towards London after the robbery, when near the turnpike road leading from Whitechurch[180] to Blandford, they experienced an apparition. A gigantic red figure seemed to stand before them resembling a woman without a head, a shawl over her shoulders, carrying an infant in her arms. The figure approached them, circled around them twice and then went away.

On Good Friday the three received the sacrament and the next day they were led from their cells to the gallows. Thomas Harvey showed no emotion, but his uncle was crying. William fainted and had to be carried to the gallows in a chair. None of them addressed the crowd, although William had prepared, in conjunction with the others, a speech which he was unable to give. It read:

---

178 *Salisbury Journal* 7/4/1823.
179 Ibid.
180 Winterborne Whitechurch.

'Good people! Mark the end of crime, and behold the awful fate of two brothers and an uncle. We confess our guilt, and acknowledge the justice of the sentence about to be executed on us. We earnestly desire to warn you against the inlets of that guilt which has brought us to an untimely and ignominious death; viz. an aversion to honest labour, and fondness for company and dissipation, a propensity to gaming, and above all the neglect of religious duties.'

For those in domestic service, he implored, 'let duty, interest and gratitude induce you to hold fast your integrity and it is our eternal wish that you take warning of our example'.

After the executions the bodies of the men were buried in St Peter's churchyard in Dorchester. Of course, it was not only the lives of the convicted that were affected by their crime. Thomas Dossiter left behind a wife and four children, Thomas Harvey a wife and one child, and William Harvey a pregnant wife and three children.

***

When Charles Brookes, butler to Sir James Dundas,[181] was told by a footman that he was going out one evening into Weymouth he thought nothing of it. It was only the next morning, at about 7.40 am, that he realised that the footman had not returned and asked the other servants if they knew where he was. One of them thought that he had gone out to bathe. About an hour later the man, who the butler knew as Edward Hamilton, had not returned, so he called the police. Thinking that something was awry he searched the house and found that several valuable items belonging to his employer were missing, including pieces of jewellery and a quantity of silver plate. He then went into the library to see if two locked dispatch cases had been taken and found that they were missing. He found them in Hamilton's room, covered with a blanket. On the floor were a hammer and a chopper. The bags had been broken into and a purse containing £30 was missing, but not the items of regalia that Admiral Dundas had been awarded throughout his illustrious naval career.

Edward Hamilton's real name was Charles Hart and it was his petty greed that was to be his downfall. He had packed the stolen items into a

181   Admiral Sir James Dundas (1785–1862) fought in the Napoleonic Wars and in 1852 led naval operations in the Black Sea.

carpet bag, which he had taken from a fellow footman, and made his way to Weymouth railway station, where he bought a ticket for London. He took a great risk by waiting there for an hour before the train arrived, but eventually he took his seat and headed for the capital, where he could lose himself in the crowds. However, his attempt to avoid observation when he bought his ticket had only led to the station master remembering him. Consequently, he was able to give the police the ticket number bought by Hart and a description.

Charles Lidbury, Superintendent of police, did not let the grass grow under his feet. He telegraphed all the railway stations between Weymouth and Paddington asking them to look out for the man, who the *Southern Times* described as 'of mild, yet moody appearance, with face devoid of moustache whisker, or beard'.[182] Guessing what the police might do, Hart interrupted his journey at Reading with the intention of transferring over to the South Eastern Railway line to continue his journey. But before he did so he went to the ticket counter and asked for a return of the difference of the fare, claiming that the staff at Weymouth had mistakenly sold him a ticket to London. Just after he left the ticket office the clerk received the telegraph, with the ticket number he had just recorded as part of the refund process. When the Reading police arrived at the South Eastern station they found their man sitting on the train, with two minutes to departure. Hart was taken into custody and admitted his guilt. He could do little else as he was carrying much of his booty with him. Also in his possession were 36 pawn tickets, for articles pledged in London and Bath, in 13 different names.

In court, the prisoner had no questions to ask the prosecution witnesses. His explanation for his crime was that during the whole time that he had worked in Weymouth he had been unwell, and it had cost him six shillings weekly for medicine. He was worried that if he complained about his health he would be dismissed, and that by selling the items it would afford him a means of subsistence until he was well. He claimed that the pawn tickets were all for his own property. The judge severely admonished Hart, then sentenced him to just thirteen months imprisonment, due to his poor health and the fact that he had already spent some time in prison.

∗∗∗

---

182   *Southern Times* 18/1/1862.

Thieving on the scale of the Milton Abbas and the Weymouth cases was not common in nineteenth century Dorset but pilfering by servants was probably quite common. On a farm at Sturminster Marshall in east Dorset, what began as a simple pilfering case turned into something more sinister, with a young girl ending up in the dock at the Lent assizes in 1856. William Martin, aged 50, farmed the 700-acre Moor Court Farm, where he lived with his wife Marselia, 20 years his junior, their three young children and five servants: a cook, two house servants, a 12-year-old nurse to the children and a groom. One of the house servants was 15-year-old Flora Everitt whom the Martins had accused of stealing a pair of stockings belonging to Marselia. She denied that she had done so, and the matter was dropped for the time being.

One morning in October, Flora was told to lay the table for breakfast. The kettle was heating on the fire and Mr Martin told her to pour the water into the teapot when it had boiled, so that his wife could pour the tea into the cups when she came downstairs. This she did, but when her mistress poured out the tea and began to drink it she said it did not taste right. When William tasted it, he found it very disagreeable and sent for the senior servant Maria Hayter. After a conversation with her, Flora was sent for and asked if she knew anything about the water, to which she said she did not. Reminding her about the affair with the stockings, William said, 'You've denied about the water; I want to know about the stockings'.[183] She twice denied knowing anything about them but on the third time of asking she admitted stealing them. At this point he called John Foote into the house, a blacksmith who happened to be working at the farm that day, to witness her confession. William told Flora that he would forgive her over the theft of the stockings, but he would not forgive her for whatever she put in the teapot. The girl stood her ground and said that she was sure that she had put nothing but water into the pot. Maria Hayter then intervened, telling Flora that she had better tell the truth. Seeing the difficulty of her situation the girl changed her story and maintained that she had put soda in the water, to which William said that was not the case because the liquid was blue, and it looked like blue vitriol. Finally, Flora admitted that it was indeed blue vitriol.[184] When the blacksmith asked her why she did it she replied that it was because her master and mistress had accused her of stealing the stockings. By now, Mrs Martin was feeling sick and had a burning sensation in her mouth. The

---

183 *Chronicle* 20/3/1856.
184 Copper sulphate – poisonous in large quantities, the symptoms of which include vomiting, headaches, convulsions and renal failure.

doctor was sent for and when he arrived he found her lying on the settee, in violent pain, caused by her ineffectual efforts to vomit. Fortunately, she eventually recovered, and the next day the local constable was called and Flora was taken into custody.

When the case came to the court Flora was charged with administering blue vitriol to her master with the intention of murdering him. Counsel for the defence contended that for the charge to be supported Mr Martin would have had to swallow some of the tea, which he did not. Given this, the prosecution said that it would agree to a verdict for attempting to administer the poison rather actually administering it. The judge, in addressing the jury, stated that it appeared that Mr Martin had not swallowed the poison, so their verdict should reflect whether they thought there was an attempt to kill him. On this charge Flora was found guilty. She was then indicted for administering poison to Mrs Martin, but no evidence was offered by the prosecution and Flora was acquitted, following a plea for mercy from the prosecution. For the original charge, the servant girl was sentenced to serve six years imprisonment with hard labour, which she served in Brixton prison.

∗∗∗

An almost identical case to that of Flora Everitt had taken place in 1854. On 26 January of that year Julia Hodder was working in her grandfather's grocery shop in Cattistock Road, Maiden Newton, a village eight miles north-west of Dorchester, when a familiar face came through the door. It was Sarah Ann Dunford from nearby Nether Kingcombe,[185] who at just 12 years old had been sent to the shop to buy some poison. She asked for some carbonate of lead[186] which was sold in packets and clearly marked poisonous, mostly bought for killing vermin. Sarah received two packets and handed over a shilling to Julia, for which she received eight-pence change. When she got back home Sarah gave the packets to Elizabeth Cornish, who had been the person who had instructed her to buy the item, telling her that it was to kill rats and mice. Sarah must have been delighted when she was given the change from the shilling on the proviso that she told nobody about the purchase.

---

185   Nether Kingcombe was a tything within the parish of Toller Porcorum.
186   Lead carbonate, white lead or cerussite – a poisonous white mineral formerly used in lead paint.

Elizabeth Cornish was a house servant to Frances Dyer Neale, the prosecutrix, and on the same afternoon the poison was bought she laid the tea table for her mistress. She placed some bread and butter on the table and some watercress. Giving evidence, Frances Neale said that when she came to the table she noticed that there was a white powder on the watercress and it tasted unpleasant. Also, her servant was most insistent that she should have a cup of tea and pointed out that the cream was very nice. Frances' suspicions may have been aroused by this kindly attitude, particularly as she had given Elizabeth notice to leave because she suspected Elizabeth was responsible for certain things going missing from the house. When the servant girl was questioned about sending out for poison she at first denied it but then admitted that she had done so and put some on a slice of bread for the mice. It was Mr Pouncy, Superintendent of police in Dorchester, who took Elizabeth into custody the day after the occurrence. The prisoner told him that at the previous Christmas she and some other servants had a lark by using lead carbonate to make them sick, and she thought she would play a trick on her mistress.

Elizabeth was 16 years old when she stood in the dock and intended to plead guilty to her crime. After all, the facts were damning; poison had been found on the bread, on the watercress, in the milk jug and in her pocket. But the judge, Mr Baron Martin, advised her against it, perhaps thinking that while the facts were indeed clear, her motives were not so obvious. Consequently, Elizabeth changed her plea to not guilty, but his words did not affect the verdict of the jury, which found her guilty of attempted poisoning. Her punishment was four years penal servitude. Having been convicted, Elizabeth was not destined to stay in Dorset but would serve her sentence in the country's capital city.

When the young girl arrived at Brixton women's prison she was no longer a prisoner but a convict and given the number 629. Brixton, which had only just reopened as a women's prison, contained around 1,100 inmates, looked after by 70 female staff who were supervised by the governor Emma Martin, who lived at the facility with her 12 children. In the prison's quarterly returns Elizabeth's health and behaviour were consistently recorded as good, which might well have influenced the decision of the authorities to transfer her to a new kind of prison.

Elizabeth had spent two years at Brixton when she was moved to a brand new and experimental facility. Fulham Women's Refuge was the brainchild of Sir Joshua Jebb, Director General of Prisons, and was part of a three-stage process to rehabilitate women. After spending time at Millbank and then Brixton, suitable convicts were sent to Fulham, where they would be taught skills to enable them to gain employment and become integrated into the wider community at the end of their term. It was called a refuge, rather than a prison or a reformatory, so as not to put off prospective employers. Unfortunately, Jebb's ideas were before their time and after his death in 1863 the facility was expanded and renamed Fulham Female Convict Prison. As for Elizabeth, after paying her dues to society she returned home to her family in Dorset.

***

Not all servants who decided to pop something extra into their employer's food or drink had injury in mind. Hannah Wright was the daughter of James Wright, who farmed 150 acres at Fontmell Magna in north Dorset. Hannah had her own business, running a small dairy which she rented from her father, and had her own house at Stour Provost. To help her she employed a 17-year-old lad, Frederick Lodge, as a yearly servant, who had been with her about twelve months.

On Wednesday 16 July 1845 Lodge found himself standing before the judge in the Shire Hall in Dorchester, facing a charge of intending to murder Hannah. One morning during the previous month, Hannah was having her breakfast when Frederick joined her and began eating his own. Then Hannah left the room for a few moments to go into the cheese room and when she returned she poured out a cup of coffee for herself, the servant having finished his breakfast and left the room. She drank some of the coffee, and finding the taste nauseous she suspected that Frederick had played some trick on her. It was when she was very sick that Hannah decided to pour out the remainder from the cup to ascertain what it was and found a dark powdered substance, which she took to Mr Buckland, the local pharmacist, who analysed the substance and found it to be cantharides.[187] Giving evidence, Henry Corbin, shop assistant of Mr Rutter, the druggist, deposed that Frederick came to the shop and asked for three pennyworth of Spanish flies, and when asked what they were for he said they were to put up a horse's nose. Frederick's defence was simple. He had no intention of harming Hannah but put the drug into her tea with the intention of making her love him. The judge told the jury that they could hardly consider that the prisoner intended to murder his mistress, however wrong he may have been. Frederick was acquitted.

---

187   A poisonous substance made from a green beetle; also known as Spanish fly.

***

A good manservant entertained a great deal of trust from his employer, but sometimes that trust was betrayed, even after a long period of employment. Colliton House in Dorchester is one of the oldest of the town's buildings.

Colliton House, built in the early 17th century, where John Guy was servant to the Churchill family. (Author copyright.)

Built by the Churchill family in the seventeenth century,[188] it remained with them until the second half of the nineteenth century. The 1841 census shows that the owner then was Rev. William Churchill, who lived there with his wife, three of his daughters and seven servants. Not listed among those living at the house was William's butler, John Guy. John had worked for William as butler for twenty years and was fortunate enough to live in a house provided by his employer, with his wife Joanna and their five children, ranging from 3 to 15 years of age. Over the years a considerable amount of trust had been established between employer and servant, but that was to be broken dramatically when William make an impromptu visit to the local butchers. Mrs Churchill had ordered some meat, in the usual manner, by giving the order to John Guy to take to William Lock, her butcher. Lock

---

188   William Churchill (1598–1690) is credited with building the existing building.

would then send her the bill for the goods and she would, each week, give money to her butler to take to the butcher in payment. In return, Lock gave Guy a signed receipt, which he took back to his mistress as proof of payment. At least, that was what should have been happening over the several years Guy had been paying the bills. But it was not so. After William Churchill had selected his meat at the butchers, he and Mr Lock entered into a conversation which put some questions in his mind about the accuracy of previous bills. When he got home he addressed the matter with Guy, but the butler's answers only aroused more suspicion. As a consequence, he took several receipted bills back to the butcher and spoke to his son Joseph; on examining one bill the butcher said that the handwriting was his sister's, except where an additional item had been added, and that the name on the bottom of the receipt was certainly his but it was not his signature.

It turned out that John Guy had been defrauding his master and mistress over several years. As far as Mrs Churchill was concerned, her meat bills were being paid weekly by Guy, but in fact he was keeping the money. The butler was clever because after several months of not paying a bill he would pay Lock just enough money to refrain him from submitting an annual account to Churchill. At the trial the butcher said that he did not chase Mr Churchill up because, being a clergyman, he was a trusted customer. However, following the conversation in the shop, Lock decided to send a letter seeking the outstanding balance.

Churchill informed the police that he suspected his butler of defrauding him and when Superintendent William Russell apprehended Guy the letter came to light. Guy had intercepted it and the policeman found it on his person, together with £48. Asked why he had prevented the letter getting to his master, he said that if he had done so he would have been discovered at once.

The extent of John Guy's fraud came out at the trial, which was held at the summer assizes of 1843. The arrest had caused great excitement and conjecture in Dorchester, to the extent that the jury were reminded that the case was a serious one and that they should dismiss from their minds all they might have previously heard on the matter and concentrate on the evidence. After listening to it they took but a minute to find the prisoner guilty of defrauding his master of over £400 over several years.[189] Addressing Guy before passing sentence, Justice Erskine said that he was guilty on two counts. The first was that, although outwardly he appeared a respectable and

189   The equivalent of over £52,000 in today's money.

trustworthy man, behind that he had perpetrated a terrible fraud. He pointed out to Guy that he was not a poor man who stole because of want; rather he had been treated with nothing but kindness by his employer's family. Neither was he someone who acted on impulse. His second crime, a most serious one, was that of forgery, for which he could show him no leniency. John Guy was sentenced to fourteen years transportation. Reporting on the trial, one newspaper pointed out that one of Guy's children, now fatherless, suffered from a disease of the hip and the leg, and further that, 'Painful as it must be to members of the Churchill family to give evidence against an old servant, we have authority to say that they consider it a duty to the public, and from which they will not flinch'.[190]

Six months after Guy's conviction an inquest was held in Millbank prison in London[191] concerning a prisoner who had been sent there pending his move to a prison hulk, before boarding a prison ship sailing to Australia. On a table in front of the coroner and the jury lay the body of John Guy. Captain Groves, the Governor of the prison, described how the prisoner was transferred to Millbank on 15 September and described him then as being very fat, with an extensive face and a florid complexion. Now, that was not the case. Now, the jury 'beheld the emaciated corpse of a fellow human being who had all the bearing of having passed 60 hard winters'.[192] The prison doctor told the court that John developed a sore throat on 1 October, which was followed by inflammation of the lungs and then of the bowels, of which he died. On returning a verdict of death by natural causes several of the jury expressed the view that there was no doubt that the bad air and the discipline of the prison hastened his death, and added that another prisoner who died previous to Guy was nothing but skin and bone, and on that occasion the doctor admitted that the fever leading to the man's death was caused by 'local issues'.

Back in Dorchester we do not know what the immediate repercussions were for John's wife Joanna and children, but we do know that tragedy visited them again when Joanna died in June 1845, leaving her children without parents. Of the five orphans, ten years later, 18-year-old Herbert was a soldier, 14-year-old Fanny, who later married, was attending a training establishment for servants in Brighton, and 12-year-old Charles was in the Dorchester workhouse.

---

190   *Warwickshire Advertiser* 20/6/1845.
191   Situated in Pimlico, Millbank prison was built as the national penitentiary and was then used as a depot for prisoners waiting to be transported.
192   *Western Flying Post* 2/12/1843.

Desperate Tragedies

In February 1852 a heavily pregnant Louisa Walborn, aged 32, turned up at a house in Coomb's Row, Allington, just to the west of Bridport, seeking accommodation. With her was 10-month old Job, one of her two illegitimate children. The *Globe* newspaper described her as 'a short woman, who possesses a countenace by no means indicative of malice; on the contrary, she has a modest and rather innocent look'.[193] The lady of the house was Mary Ann Sheppick who took on the new lodger at a rent of one shilling a week and gave her an upstairs room looking over the lane. Louisa was from Thorncombe, about ten miles to the north-west of Bridport, where she married Stephen Walborn in 1845, giving birth to a son John the following year. However, the couple had parted, and she lived for some time with a man named James White. She then left him and went to live with her parents in her home village, before moving to Bridport.

One factor that might have encouraged Mary Ann to take on Louise was that the woman looked as if she could pay her rent; she was reasonably dressed and had plenty of clothes. She may also have had some sympathy for Louisa's situation, having an illegitimate child of her own. In court, Mary Ann admitted that she had lived with a number of men and one of her daughters had had a 'love child'.[194] Her occupation was given as spinner, but she also said, 'I have got my living from doing something that is wrong',[195] and divulged that a man visited one of her lodgers on a regular basis. Then, there was an occasion when she had been accused of picking a man's pocket of £10 but was discharged when the accuser did not turn up at court, having been paid off with £5 by her sister. Despite all this, widow Mary Ann seems to have settled down to a normal family life with her four children, earning her living by letting rooms.

Ten weeks after Louisa moved into her new accommodation she showed signs of giving birth. What happened next was disclosed by various witnesses at an inquest, held at the Plymouth Inn, Allington, on 5 May. Mary Ann told the coroner's court that on realising that Louisa was about to give birth she sent for the midwife, Mary Hine, a lady experienced in her vocation. The birth took about forty minutes without complications, and the result, according to the midwife, was 'a fine, healthy male child'. She then washed

193   *Globe* 21/5/1852.
194   *London Evening Mail* 26/7/1852.
195   Ibid.

the newborn, checked him over and dressed him. Next, she gave him some butter and sugar, as was usual at the time. Lastly, she gave the new baby to his mother and left the house.

Whilst Mrs Hine was caring for the mother, Mary Ann and her daughter Elizabeth kept an eye on Louisa's other child and then began to prepare tea. About twenty minutes after the midwife had left the two women heard three cries coming from the baby and when Elizabeth entered Louisa's room she asked her what the matter was. Louisa replied that the child appeared to be sick. Picking up the infant, Elizabeth noticed that there was a black mark at the corner of its mouth, so she took it to her mother. Mary Ann could see immediately that all was not as it should be, the mouth of the child was burnt, so she asked Louisa if she had hurt her baby. An emphatic no was the reply, but there had been no one else in the house and she was sure that neither the midwife nor her daughter had harmed the child. In court Mary Ann said that Louisa's general behaviour before and during the confinement gave no indication of being incoherent or wild. Louisa's bed was up against a wall by a window and it did occur to Mary Ann that she may have thrown something out into the lane.

Concerned at the baby's condition Mary Ann decided to call Mrs Hine back again. As soon as the midwife saw the infant she had a strong suspicion that it had been given oil of vitriol.[196] She had recently burnt her finger after spilling some on it, and it had turned black like the mouth of the child. Confronting the mother Mrs Hine asked her what she had given her baby. 'Nothing', she said. Mrs Hine called her a liar and said that it looked like oil of vitriol, to which Louisa said nothing. The police and a doctor were sent for, both of whom gave evidence at Louisa's trial.

PC Edward Brookes testified that on the evening of 5 May he had been sent for. Arriving at the house he found the prisoner lying in bed and after searching the room he found nothing suspicious, but noticing that the bed was near the window he decided to look around outside. There he found a cork and a small glass bottle, which he later gave to Dr Allen. He noticed also that some of the leaves under the bushes where he found the items were burnt. Another witness, Fanny Welch, deposed that the baby had been put into her care overnight with strict instructions from the police not to let anyone near it. Throughout the night it had convulsions and the following day died. Dr Allen described to the court in detail the condition of the child when he examined it. His conclusions were that it had died by being given

---

196 Hydrous copper sulphate, which was used as a stain remover in laundry.

oil of vitriol and that the bottle found by PC Brookes had contained the same substance. In his opinion death could not have been caused by natural causes.

With such a mountain of evidence against Louisa, and the fact that twenty-three out of twenty-four of the jurors at the inquest had agreed a verdict of 'wilful murder', Mr Stock, for the defence, did not attempt to discredit the witnesses. Instead, he brought forward Samuel Aplin, a clothier, who said he had known the prisoner for sixteen years and that she was very humane to her two other children. Stock then addressed the jury, telling them often in cases like this, shame was the motivation for murder, but it did not apply to Louisa as she already had an illegitimate child. Neither was poverty a cause. He suggested to the jury that the questions they had to consider were whether the child had been poisoned and whether or not the prisoner had administered it to the deceased? In his view there was no proof that she had bought any poison.

It was now time for the judge, Mr Baron Martin, to sum up. He told the jury that if they had any uncertainty then they would have to give the prisoner the benefit of the doubt. However, if they found the evidence conclusive they should not let any other consideration affect them and find her guilty. It was murder or nothing. The jury retired and after a short period returned to the courtroom. The briefness of their deliberations was not surprising to those present, given the damning evidence against the prisoner. What did surprise them was their decision. The foreman stood up and pronounced a not guilty verdict. Members of the public were shocked at the decision and one woman was heard to say, as she left the court, 'I'll get rid of my young _____ [sic] now', and another, 'We need not care what we do now'.[197]

∗∗∗

The case of Louisa Walborn was not the only trial of child murder in 1852 to provoke a reaction from those present in court. A case held in March of the same year caused a reporter of the *Taunton Courier* and *Western Advertiser* to write that he had been present at one of the saddest scenes he had ever witnessed – a case where the accused were overwhelmed with grief, as was the audience, and even the judge shed tears at times. He was referring to

---

197   *London Evening Mail* 26/7/1852.

the trial of Frances Taylor, accused of murdering her infant child. Also in the dock were Jane Taylor, Frances's mother, her aunt Ann Prouse, and the father of the child, Richard Paul, whom Frances was due to marry. They were charged with harbouring Frances after the fact. All of the prisoners pleaded not guilty.

The previous October, Sexton William Amey went to St George's church, Fordington. In the porch he found a wooden box containing the corpse of a male child which had a bruise on its head. The box also contained a half crown and a piece of paper upon which was written 'A dead baby; please put it under ground'. Two days later Rev. Henry Moule[198] received an anonymous letter which took him to the house of Frances (Fanny) Taylor. The first person to see him was Frances's mother, who said, 'I suppose you have come about the child – Fanny is the mother of it'. Fanny told him that the child had been born dead, adding that when it was born it fell and hit its head against the leg of the table. In court Moule said that he had known the family for many years and had no reason to think that they might harm a child. Richard Paul told the jury that he would have given anything for the child to have lived, but, as it was dead, he made a wooden box and put the note inside it, before taking it to the church.

Surgeon John Colston carried out the post-mortem and found that the physiological condition of the body suggested that the infant was living independently when it died of a blow to the head or a fall from a great height. In his address to the jury the judge advised that they first had to decide whether the child was born alive and then whether Frances had killed her. The jury found the prisoners not guilty and they were discharged. But, while the justice system had finished with them, some people were not. As they left the court they were followed by a mob, chiefly consisting of women, who harangued them all the way to their homes.

If certain newspapers were to be believed, Dorset was a hotbed of immorality. The *London Times* ran an article in which it said, 'The county of Dorset has for some time obtained an evil notoriety in consequence of the practice of child murder, which has obtained to a lamentable extent among the younger female population of that county'. Speaking of the jury in the Walborn case, it had no hesitation in condemning them, saying,

'We can scarcely congratulate the jurors on the result of their labours. Thus, impunity has been conceded – at least in the County of Dorset – to a crime well

---

198   Henry Moule MA (1801–1880) became the incumbent at St George's church, Fordington, in 1829 and remained in the post until his death. Unpopular at first because of his evangelical approach he became a prominent person in the town because of his attempts at improving the conditions of the poor, especially with regard to sanitary conditions. His own contribution to improved sanitation took a practical form; he invented the earth closet.

nigh the most dreadful in the dismal catalogue of crimes. Whether we consider the victims, or the terrible fact of the wholesale extinction of life, or the demoralising effect upon the offenders themselves, we shall have equal reason to be dissatisfied with the Dorchester jury. They have set a premium on spontaneous concubinage; they have inoculated a district with the habits of crime; they have embedded human life with a slight account in the eyes of an ignorant population. There is little doubt that a plentiful crop of child murder will be the natural consequence of this verdict during the ensuing autumn.'[199]

The *Morning Advertiser* clearly put the blame for the prevalence of infanticide in Dorset not on the leniency of juries but on the Poor Law Amendment Act of 1834. According to that newspaper, the Act encouraged and even prompted mothers to kill their children, because of the unfairness of its provisions. Under the previous Poor Law Act, passed in 1576, it had been ordered that bastard children should be supported by their reputed father and under a 1732 provision a mother who was pregnant with an illegitimate child was required to declare under oath who the father was. He would then be tracked down and imprisoned until he agreed to maintain his offspring. It would be nice to think that the intention of this law was to protect the mother from the burden of bringing up her child on her own, but, in fact, it was to ensure that the parish did not incur the expense of maintaining them. The 1834 Act swept away the existing laws and in doing so completely took away the father's responsibility. From then on it became the sole duty of the mother to bring up her illegitimate child until he or her was 16 years old. If a woman was unable to support her child, then they would both have to go into the workhouse.

The *Southern Times* took another view, directing its criticism not at the jury or the Poor Law but at the punishment. In an article headed 'Human Kittens and Blind Puppies', it wrote, not without sarcasm, that,

'Among the female fashions for the present season, the assize reports indicate infanticide as very prevalent. One Louisa Walford, indicted at Dorchester assizes for the murder of her little boy, was acquitted on evidence so conclusive – if true – of her guilt, and after a summing up so decidedly against her, that the jury either thought the witnesses perjurers, and the judge a blockhead, or have looked upon the child as a flea or a rat .... Soon in Dorsetshire we shall have maternal affection displaying itself at the druggists' counter, by requests for strychnine and prussic acid, "Just to poison the babies". [200]

199 *London Times*, quoted in *Salisbury and Winchester Journal* 31/7/1854.
200 *Southern Times* 8/8/1852.

The newspaper went on to contend that the reason juries were retuning not guilty verdicts where the evidence was overwhelmingly against the accused was that if they convicted, the judge was obliged to pass a death sentence. The answer, in the paper's view, was to abolish hanging for this crime and it suggested transportation would be the better option.[201]

***

Fortunately, not all cases involving babies ended in tragedy. One mother who might well have found herself on trial for infanticide was 21-year-old Louiza Morris, had it not been for an alert member of the public. Louiza, who was not married, had been living in Southampton as a servant girl, where she gave birth to a baby boy. She was travelling by train to her home in Broadwey, just north of Weymouth, when she interrupted her journey. Alighting from the train either at Wool or Moreton railway station, she took the child, who was just 5 weeks old, and left him in a shallow ditch by the turnpike. He was wrapped up in flannel, but given it was the beginning of February he was unlikely to survive for very long. It was Thomas Saunders who found the babe the following day, who took it to a Mrs Parker who told the court that there was nothing wrong with the baby and it began to feed heartily. Louiza was the first woman to be convicted under a new statute which stated that 'any person who shall abandon or expose any child under two years of age, whereby the life of such a child shall be endangered, or the health shall have been, or likely to be, permanently injured'[202] would be guilty of a misdemeanour. Before this statute actual injury had to be proved, but now intention became the crux of the matter. The judge, in delivering the sentence, said that he did not believe Louiza intended to take away the life of her child, and sentenced her to six months imprisonment.

---

201   In fact, transportation was stopped the following year.
202   *Chronicle* 13/3/1862.

A Question of Sanity

By 7.30 am on the morning of 27 March 1863 a large crowd, estimated to be between 4,000 and 5,000, had gathered in the water meadows to the north of Dorchester. The *London Times* noted that the majority of them seemed to be women of the lower orders who had been streaming into the town for the whole of the night. Above and in front of them was the high wall of Dorchester gaol, and above that could be seen the north entrance of the prison. They were about to witness a double hanging and Dorchester's last public execution. The two men concerned were Charles Fooks and Edwin Preedy.

Charles, a 49-year-old farmer living at Walditch, situated about a mile outside the town of Bridport, was a bachelor living with his two nieces, Martha Hallett and Jane Fooks. He had some standing and respect in the community and had been a way warden and overseer.[203]

At about 7.30 am on the morning of 29 August 1862 William Parker was walking along the road near Charles Fooks' house when he saw the farmer come out of his front door carrying a shotgun. Daniel Stone, Fooks' cousin, had just passed the property when Parker saw Fooks approach him from behind and from about four yards deliberately shoot the man in the back of the head. The assailant then calmly went back indoors, where shortly after the sound of another shot was heard.

John Bishop was working in his garden and when he heard the first shot he went to investigate, finding Stone in the road with blood coming from his head. Cradling the man in his arms he spoke to him but got no reply. Then, with two short breaths Stone died. William Shepherd, a brush maker, was also working in his garden opposite Fooks' house and heard both shots. Of course, it was not unusual for gunshots to be heard in a farming community but, he said, the second shot was unlike the first, more of a muffled sound. When he went into the street he found a number of people standing around Fooks' house, so he and a man called Adams decided to investigate. The back door of the house was open, but when they went upstairs they found the bedroom door locked. Shepherd went outside and found a ladder and climbed up to the bedroom window. Looking through it he saw Fooks on the floor by the bed with a shotgun lying next to him. After the bedroom door was broken open Shepherd went into the room where he found that the

---

203   Voluntary posts associated with the maintenance of roads.

prostrate casualty had been wounded in the lip and the forehead but he was alive. As he raised the wounded man from the floor he was asked, 'Is the other one dead? I hope he is.' The police were sent for, and after ascertaining what had gone on, Constable Lavender charged Fooks with murder. He replied, 'He has teased me long enough. I have been very nervous for the last month.'[204]

From evidence given at the trial it was apparent that the prisoner and the deceased had not been on good terms for some time, despite attempts by relatives to bring the two cousins together. For instance, Stone's brother-in-law Richard Garland, who was also a long-term friend of the two men, had tried to patch things up between them after a vestry meeting. He suggested that as they were all friends they should give up any old grievance, although just what the grievance was all about nobody seemed to know. Stone agreed that they should shake hands but Fooks flatly refused to do so. Confirming the relationship, one witness, Daniel Read, claimed that he had heard Fooks say that if he ever caught his

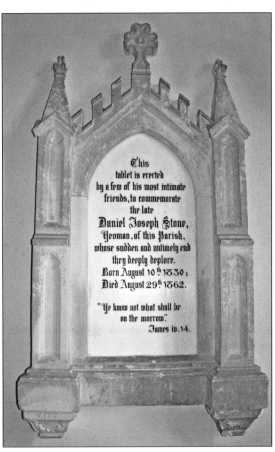

Memorial to Daniel Stone, St Mary's church, Walditch. (Author copyright.)

cousin on his property he would shoot him like a rook, a statement that caused some reaction from the crowd in the courtroom. Commenting on the prisoner's behaviour, Read told the jury that occasionally the prisoner had complained of pains in the head and would say, 'Oh dear, it is so bad I don't know what you are saying to me or me to you'. He also remarked to him, 'I would not mind shooting a dozen men, perhaps I should shoot myself'.[205]

Addressing the jury for the defence, Mr Coleridge said that he would not insult their understanding of the facts, but that this was an extraordinary case and while the act was not in question the defence was that the prisoner was not in a right state of mind when he did what he did. He next furnished the jury with instances of previous cases, similar to this one, where acquittals had been given because of unsound mind. The law's view of insanity as a defence in criminal cases had been established by the M'Naghten Rule. This stated that to establish a defence on the ground of insanity it must be clearly proved that at the time of committing the act the party accused was labouring under such a defect of reason, from disease of the mind, as not to know the nature and quality of the act he was doing; or if he did know it, that he did not know he was doing wrong.

Martha Hallett, Fooks' niece and witness for the defence, attested that on several occasions her uncle had told her to put the shutters up for he fancied that Stone was outside listening to what they were saying. She also said that sometimes her uncle was rather strange, often complaining of pains in his head and of nervousness. If she smiled at him, he would say she was laughing at him. The day before the killing Martha left his house because lately his behaviour had deteriorated and she was frightened of him.

It was now the turn of Dr Thomas Harrington Tuke,[206] an eminent physician who specialised in psychiatry and who had been brought down from London to give evidence. Tuke told the court that he had spoken to Fooks in the gaol, in the presence of the medical officer and the deputy governor. The prisoner had spoken freely about the event saying that he had no idea that he could hurt anyone and when asked if he thought he was deranged he answered, 'Oh, no, no, sir; I baint mad',[207] adding that he knew he did it but not why he did it. Asked to give an instance where Stone had harmed or offended him Fooks could not think of one, but when pressed said, 'Well, I was once told an acre and a half of one of my fields had been

205   Ibid.
206   Dr Thomas Harrington Tuke FRPCE FRCP (1826–1888) took over the running of a private asylum in Chiswick, following the death of his father. He contributed towards the Victorian policy on lunacy, advocating a more humane approach, like letting patients walk around freely rather than being restrained.
207   *Sherborne Mercury* 17/3/1863.

planted with docks,[208] and sure enough there it was and Stone might have done it'.[209] Tuke's conclusion, based on his forty-five-minute interview with the accused, was that at the time of the shooting he was of unsound mind and that he had a malady that rendered nugatory any effort of self-control. Citing one aspect of the prisoner's behaviour, he said that insane people often think that people are laughing and jeering at them. Asked by the judge if in his view when Fooks raised the gun at Stone did he think it would kill him, the witness replied that at the time he believed he did, but that pulling the trigger was the natural promptings of the mind he could not control.

An opposing medical view was given by Dr Good, surgeon at the gaol. He testified that he had visited Fooks two or three times a week whilst he was in prison and could find no reason to conclude that from what he saw the prisoner was insane. He accepted that he had not read the standard works on insanity and explained that his study of it had not come from the reading of books but through common sense. According to him, after conversing with a man not much skill is required to come to the truth of his sanity. Dr Curme, another surgeon, told the court that he had also visited the prisoner briefly on a couple of occasions and never saw any indications of suicide or homicide. In an attempt to put things into perspective the defence counsel, in his final remarks, pointed out that the latter evidence did not contravene that of Dr Tuke who had twenty years of studying cases of delusion and insanity, whilst they had no knowledge of the science.

In his summing up Judge Shee told the jury that to establish the defence of insanity it must be proved clearly to their satisfaction that at the time he did the act he was under a defect of reason as not to know the nature of the deed he was doing and he didn't know it was wrong. To labour under the delusion that another person was doing you some personal injury was not sufficient ground for murder. After asking for permission to retire the jury took just fifteen minutes to come back with a guilty verdict. A reporter at the trial wrote that the judge was visibly affected when passing the sentence of death. As throughout the trial, the prisoner maintained an indifference and then walked passively from the dock.

As soon as the outcome of the trial was made public a debate ensued about the verdict and strenuous efforts were made to get the sentence remitted. Rev. Templar wrote a letter to the *London Times* in which he said that after an acquaintance of fifteen years with the prisoner he had never known a

---

208 Weeds.
209 *Sherborne Mercury* 17/3/1863.

man more insane as a sane man nor sane as an insane man as Fooks.[210] Lord Wynford, Fooks' landlord, wrote to Sir George Grey, the Home Secretary, seeking mercy. The chaplain of Dorchester prison, Rev. Watson, also wrote and then took the matter further by going up to London and laying the facts before the authorities. The Home Secretary's view of the case was contained in a reply to Watson's plea. It read: 'I am directed by Secretary Sir George Grey to acknowledge the receipt of your letter of 18 instant, regarding Charles Fooks, now under sentence of death. In reply I am to state that all the facts of the case having been before the jury, who had also had an opportunity of hearing and considering the medical evidence of the state of the prisoner's mind, and the law having been clearly laid down by the judge, Sir George Grey cannot act against their deliberate verdict and that the opinion you have formed that the prisoner's mind is diseased is not a sufficient ground for interfering with the verdict.'[211]

Also, articles questioning the verdict began to appear in the press and even the respected medical journal *The Lancet* felt obliged to comment, saying,

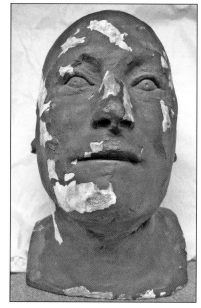

'To carry out the sentence of death would be to accomplish a cruel judicial murder' and that 'To hang this unhappy man would be an act of horrible and senseless cruelty, from which science and common sense revolt'.[212] Despite the petitions and criticisms, Grey dismissed them all, declaring that he saw no reason why the sentence should not go ahead. On being told this and the date of his trial Fooks reportedly sighed and said, 'Oh dear!'

While awaiting his fate the condemned man spent a great deal of time with the prison chaplain, in prayer and talking about his crime. He told him that he hoped that God would forgive him for what he had done but added that he really looked upon Stone as his killer, and that they would both meet in heaven. He also asked the chaplain to write to his

A plaster cast of Charles Fooks' head. (Courtesy of Dorset Museum.)

210   Quoted in *Salisbury Journal* 21/3/1863.
211   Letter from the Home Office dated 19/3/1863.
212   *Western Gazette* 31/3/1863.

wife in Burton Bradstock, telling her that he hoped that they would meet in heaven. Fooks did not confess to his crime but maintained that he had no more power to help himself that day than a child. He also wanted to give a warning to those who did not care how they jeered and teased others and drove them mad for their sport.

✱✱✱

If Charles Fooks was quiet and sullen throughout his trial the same could not be said of Edwin Preedy. If the various witnesses at his trial were to be believed, the 20 year old standing before the judge had already had an irregular upbringing: sometimes in the union workhouse and on one occasion in a reformatory, from which he ran away. According to his mother, as a child he had fallen and banged his head badly, when he was hit by his step-father, an event the *Southern Times* described as considerably exaggerated.[213] Stories about his pedigree and upbringing began to circulate. One was that his father had been a clerk working in Warwickshire who had become a tradesman and a lay preacher; another that his mother took him to London where he became a 'city Arab'.[214]

In January 1859 Preedy was given four months hard labour in Warwick gaol for stealing a gallon of apples, valued at sixpence.[215] His next period of incarceration was in Carmarthen prison where he spent ten weeks for larceny, and it was whilst there that it was discovered that he was a deserter from the 85th Regiment of Foot. Faced with returning to the army, Edwin displayed the violent side of his character that would re-emerge later, attacking the warders and exclaiming that he would swing for someone rather than return to soldiering.

Preedy's next waymark on his route to Dorchester assizes was Haverford West, where he was arraigned on three separate charges for stealing various items of clothing. The sentence given was three years penal servitude, which provoked a parting remark from him to the judge of 'Thank you, sir'.[216] If the authorities thought that this severe punishment would tame the young 19 year old they were mistaken. His character in prison was described as 'not

213 *Southern Times* 28/3/1863.
214 Ibid.
215 Warwick Quarter sessions 4/1/1859.
216 *Potters Electric News* 10/7/1861.

This illustration dated 1848 shows a convict eating his meal in his cell at Portland prison. (Copyright Illustrated London News/*Mary Evans Picture Library.)*

good', and consequently he was transferred to Millbank prison, where he was reported for idleness and flogged for striking a warder. In March 1861 Edwin was sent to Portland to undertake his penal servitude in the quarries and it was there that he attacked a warder, resulting in him appearing at the 1863 Lent assizes. When he was asked to plead at his trial, he replied, 'I did the act, but not intentionally, sir'. The Clerk of Arraigns told him that he must plead guilty or not guilty, to which Preedy answered, 'If it is a matter of form, I say not guilty, sir'.

The first witness was a fellow convict, John Moore, who described what had happened on 8 September of the previous year. He was part of a cleaning gang whose job it was to go around the cells with a warder after dinner and collect the metal food tins and knives used by the prisoners.

On that day he was doing the round with warder Charles and two other convicts, named Ashton and Schofield. When they reached Preedy's cell Evans unlocked the door and Schofield put his hand out for the knife. Preedy pushed him to one side and rushed at the warder, holding him with one hand while stabbing him just under the ear with the other, killing him. The two convicts seized the prisoner and it was then that he dropped the knife. What happened in the court room next was described graphically by a reporter who was there:

'At this moment a fearful scene took place. When the accused first came to the bar he looked a very harmless young man, but during the evidence he became restless, and sharply asked a question. Immediately after the answer the prisoner threw one leg and arm over the front of the dock, and very nearly succeeded in getting over. Two warders who were in the dock rushed and seized him, and other warders jumped into the dock, and an almost deadly struggle took place, the prisoner kicking, fighting, and roaring more like a wild beast than a human being, and it required nearly ten strong men to hold him. Several had hold of his arms and his legs and some were holding him by his hair and his head. This continued for some minutes, and when it ceased it was only because he was held fast. The ferocity of the man was beyond anything that can be imagined.'[217]

Judge Shee then intervened, asking the prison surgeon, who had gone over to Preedy, if he felt that his state of mind allowed the trial to continue. He responded by saying that in his opinion the prisoner was sensible to all that was going on, and he asked the prisoner directly if he knew him. 'Of course, I do, shake hands. You are a friend of mine' was the reply. This dialogue

---

217   *Gloucester Chronicle* 14/3/1863.

brought on another bout of violence and it was suggested to the judge that the man be put in irons. Reluctantly, he agreed and Preedy was now confined in irons and heavy straps. Next, Judge Shee decided to seek some advice on how to proceed and consulted with his colleague Justice Byles. On his return into the court Shee found that the prisoner's demeanour had changed completely. He looked exhausted and he was acting as if asleep. The judge ordered him to be taken to a room for examination and after about half an hour the trial resumed.

James Douglas, assistant warder at Portland, was the next person to testify, saying that he had asked Preedy why he had killed Evans, but he did not seem to have had a reason, except to say that there was something between him and the warder nobody knew about. Superintendent George Underwood had the job of taking the prisoner to Dorchester gaol. On the journey they passed some street clowns and Preedy laughed at them. Given the situation, Underwood asked him if he was not concerned about his plight, to which he answered that it was important that he kept his spirits up. He also said that he was sorry that he had killed the man, as the warders told him that he was a good sort and had a large family. He claimed that he had a grudge against all of the warders and that day he decided to kill the first that came near him.

The governor of Dorchester prison described how whilst awaiting trial the man's behaviour went from one extreme to the other. When he first arrived he was extremely violent, breaking up everything and tearing his own clothes, which led them to put him in solitary confinement, naked, for two days. When he had calmed down he was put with others to prevent him harming himself, and he began to show a gentler side of his character. For example, Edwin caught three sparrows in the exercise yard, one of which was injured. He looked after them in his cell, and when the injured one died he showed great sorrow.

As in the Fooks case, the facts of what had happened were unquestionable. The matter to be considered by the jury was the prisoner's state of mind. Unlike the Fooks case there was no eminent surgeon giving evidence and the court had to rely on the judgement of local doctors, all of whom said that in their opinion there was no reason to think him insane.

Mr Prideaux opened the case for the defence by reading out a statement made by Preedy in which he claimed that the murdered man had tyrannized him and told him that his mother lay dying and that he had murdered her, and that this had driven him mad. Addressing the court Prideaux made the best defence he could for his client, suggesting that his behaviour in the court was that of a mad man, and if it was not then he must be the most accomplished actor that ever lived. He also pointed out the prisoner's gentleness to those who were kind to him and that he had shown tender love to the sparrows.

In an effort to show cause for his action Edwin's mother was brought to the stand. She declared that as a four-year-old he had an accident to his head which affected his behaviour, followed by being beaten on the head at school. Just then his mother stopped, turned towards her son and collapsed, exclaiming, 'Oh, my poor son'. This led to another bout of violence from Preedy, which was managed by the three men holding him. The mother's testimony was corroborated by Mary Smith, an aunt.

It did not take the jury long to return a verdict of guilty, which the judge fully concurred with. Then, an unfortunate occurrence happened outside the court. It was the day of the wedding between the Prince of Wales and Princess Alexandra of Denmark and in celebration the bells of St Peter's church began to ring a merry tune. The Under-Sheriff was sent out of the court to put a stop to it and the judge continued with the death sentence. This time there were no histrionics and the prisoner silently left the court room.

Back in the prison Edwin Preedy reverted to being violent and uncooperative, refusing to take any spiritual guidance or make a confession. Then he changed, the catalyst for which was Rev. Henry Moule.[218] Under his guidance Edwin began to pray and seek solace in God. The degree of Moule's influence can be measured by the statement he managed to get Preedy to write and wanted read out at his execution. In it he regretted his crime and his behaviour toward those who tried to help him while he was awaiting his punishment. Regarding his sanity, he declared that he had never been mad except from passion: 'Pride, passion and low life will account for all the wild actions of my life', he declared. His advice to others was to shun places of temptation and evil company. Children, he said, should try with prayer to restrain from pride and passion.

At 8 am on the day of the executions the prison bell began its mournful toll. About fifteen minutes before that, behind the scenes of the drama, the Under-Sheriff arrived at the prison with a group of javelin men. In accordance with tradition, he knocked on the door of the prison, and in response to the question of who was there he replied that on behalf of the Sheriff he had come to demand the bodies of Charles Fooks and Edwin Alfred Preedy. Shortly afterwards Calcraft the executioner was called for, and the party entered the north-east wing of the prison where the pinioning was to take place.

---

218   Moule produced a pamphlet about his work with Preedy entitled *Hope Against Hope.*

Fooks and Preedy met for the first time in the prison yard. Preedy shook the hands of the Under-Sheriff, Governor and Calcraft. He then removed from a finger a ring made of beads which he presented to the executioner as a gift, an act perhaps conveying an acknowledgement that the executioner was just doing his job. The solemn procession made its way to the gate of the prison and both men ascended the steps accompanied by Rev. Moule. Once on the roof of the lodge, the two men shook hands and those of the attendants. The caps and ropes were then fitted and, to the background of Rev. Templar reading from *Psalms*, Calcraft withdrew the bolts and the two men fell to their doom. An hour after, the bodies were taken down and placed in coffins, in which they would be buried later in the day, within the precincts of the gaol. Most of the crowd stayed until the end, perhaps expecting some drama from Preedy, but they were disappointed. In fact, the prison authorities had erected some scaffolding around the platform in case he attempted to jump off. Both men died with dignity, which is not a word that could be attributed to the crowd on the day. The *Salisbury Journal* reported

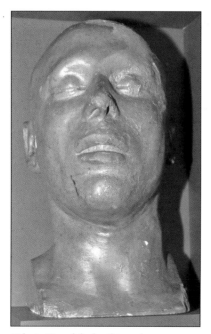

Edwin Preedy's death mask. (Courtesy of Dorset Museum.)

that, 'For some time after the executions the streets of the town presented the appearance of a fair … many of the men were in such a state as did not speak much for the moral teaching of public executions'.[219] One story, related by Rev. Filleul, is that two enterprising brothers erected a grandstand in the water meadows, charging two and sixpence a seat. Unfortunately, the weight of the audience was too much, and it collapsed, sinking into the soft soil. A macabre postscript to the story can be found in Bradford Peverell school logbook, which contains the following entry, dated 27 March 1863: 'Some of the children went to Dorchester to see Mr Fooks and Mr Preedy hung.' Below it is another note which reads, 'They should not have gone, had I known it and been able to prevent them. H. B. W.'[220]

219   *Salisbury Journal* 28/3/1863.
220   Dorset Ancestors.

***

Four months after the Fooks and Preedy trials the question of insanity arose again at the 1863 summer assizes.

According to many, including his son John, Henry Dommett, a 50-year-old hemp sorter living in Allington, Bridport, had always been a loving man towards his wife and six children. Mary Marshallsay, a neighbour, claimed that he was 'a very, very tender father and husband – never a better in England'.[221] He was also shy and devout in his religion. Then people noticed a change in his behaviour. He became depressed and nervous, and sought solitude. Instead of going into his garden when he came home from work, which he usually did, he went into the back room of the house and sat alone or went to bed. According to his son, the change began a few months before his trial, when he became increasingly excited, sometimes depressed, and often refusing to speak to his children.

Despite this behaviour nothing could prepare the family for what happened on 5 June 1863. That morning John was upstairs in his parents' house when he was disturbed by a noise. He called to his father but got no answer and likewise called to his young brother Charles, with the same result. So he went down to the pantry, where saw his father and brother, aged six. The boy was lying on the floor with his throat cut, and his father sat in a nearby chair. John exclaimed, 'Oh, father what have you done?' but he got no reply. After his mother was called some neighbours were summoned, and the child was carried out of the room. One of the neighbours, Ester Keech, told the jury that she went back into the pantry and said to Henry Dommett, 'Poor man, I am sure you did not intend to hurt your child'. He made no reply but drew up his arms and legs and began shaking violently. Then, he pointed to two spots of blood on his trousers and asked, 'Is he dead?' The neighbour assured him that his son was not, to which Dommett remarked, 'He must die'.[222] Charles actually died a few minutes after the incident. Dommett was arrested by Constable Lavender, the same policeman who had arrested Charles Fooks, and taken to Dorchester gaol.

At Dommett's trial Justice Willes reminded the grand jury, when addressing them, that when deciding if the prisoner had a case to answer for they had to consider just the facts and not take account of any mitigating circumstances

---

221 *Southern Times* 25/7/1863.
222 *Salisbury Journal* 25/7/1863.

like the condition of the prisoner's mind, as that was the job of the petty jury. The prisoner standing in the dock who was described as 'a short, quiet-looking man, with nothing of the murderous about his countenance, after some hesitation, pleaded not guilty'.[223] Several witnesses were called for the prosecution, each describing Dommett's deteriorating behaviour. Of the medical testaments presented, one was that of Dr John Good, surgeon at the prison. He had interviewed the prisoner on several occasions and had concluded that at the time the crime was committed he was suffering from homicidal mania and did not know what he was doing.

After listening to all the witnesses, it took just five minutes for the jury to conclude that Henry Dommett was not guilty by way of insanity. He was sentenced to be detained at Her Majesty's pleasure and was sent to Fisherton lunatic asylum.[224]

***

Another trial involving a father and his child took place at the 1831 summer assizes. Job Nobbs and his wife Elizabeth lived in Cattistock, a village eight miles north-west of Dorchester. Mrs Nobbs gave birth to a baby boy in March 1831, but soon afterwards became very ill and died on 11 April. Mary Legg, giving evidence for the prosecution, told the court that she went into the house while her aunt was ill to help out and look after the newborn. On the afternoon of the day the offence was committed Mary made some bread pap[225] for the infant who was too weak to eat it all, so she left the remainder on the dresser to be consumed later. It was established that the prisoner came home from work at about 5 pm. At about 8 pm it was time for the baby to be fed again, but instead of using the remainder of the bread pap Mary decided to prepare biscuit pap, as it was easier to digest. Later that evening a relative, Mrs Wightman, came to see Mrs Nobbs and while she was there the baby started crying, so she took it downstairs to feed it. Seeing what was left from the earlier feed she picked up the cup from the dresser, noticing that it smelt rather strong. She then asked Mary Legg if she had added something to it, which she denied.

---

223   *Chronicle* 30/7/1863.
224   Fisherton House asylum, Fisherton Anger, Wiltshire, accepted criminal lunatics until 1870, a few years after Broadmoor was established.
225   Soft or semi-liquid food for infants.

Mrs Wightman decided to take the baby to her home to feed it there, but when she returned to the Nobbs house she got quite a shock from Job who asked her 'whether the young son of a b_____h [sic] was not dead, as he thought he had been long ago'.[226] She was now suspicious of Nobbs, particularly as she had heard him say on a previous occasion that he was worried his wife would die and the child would live to plague him, and on another, that the child was not his and he would not own it. Mrs Wightman had saved the cup of pap and it was sent to Dorchester for analysis, where it was confirmed that it contained enough laudanum to kill a small child. On being asked if there was any laudanum in the house Nobbs denied that there was, which was clearly a lie because the local pharmacist confirmed that he had bought some a few days earlier. For the defence, Mary Drew declared that she had heard Nobbs say that he should be very fond of the child if it should please God to let the mother live to take care of it. The child died ten days after his mother.

Nobbs was accused of attempting to administer a quantity of laudanum to his son Philip with the intention of murdering him. It took the jury just a few minutes to bring in a guilty verdict. In his address to the prisoner Judge Alderson said, 'I cannot under such circumstances as these, venture to hold out to you any reasonable hope of mercy being extended to you this side of the grave; and it is my duty – my bound and solemn duty – to call on you now to remember your latter and which is soon to approach, to spend a few days which you are allotted you in this world in preparation for your departure to eternity … and though I cannot recommend you to the mercy of the Crown, yet I do recommend you to the mercy of your god.'[227] The *Chronicle* went on to inform its readers that the judge was much affected when he pronounced the death sentence, as were those present in the court, except for the prisoner, whose conduct throughout the trial was described as strangely apathetic.

Despite Justice Alderson's words Nobbs did not hang. Following representations to the Home Secretary by John Frampton, a solicitor from Cerne Abbas, his sentence was commuted to transportation for life. Fifty-two-year-old Nobbs was sent to the convict hulk *Captivity*[228] before joining 223 other convicts on board the ship *Isabella*, bound for New South Wales. The journey to Australia was not without incident. During a short stop in

226 *Sherborne Mercury* 25/7/1831.
227 *Chronicle* 28/7/1831.
228 The *Captivity* began life as *HMS Bellerophon* and served as a prison hulk from 1815 to 1836.

Plymouth a soldier overheard some convicts saying that they would gladly take an opportunity to take over the ship, which led to all of them being put into double irons for a considerable time. Trouble was not confined to the convicts. An incident on board began when one of the ship's crew, Jacob Anderson, refused to obey an order to hang up a clothesline for the convicts to dry their clothes on. He was put into the poop but escaped and went onto the foredeck. On hearing the noise Thomas Galloway,[229] ship's surgeon, came up onto the quarter deck where he witnessed the second mate, who was trying to apprehend Anderson, being pushed around by some of the crew. It was not long before the military guard arrived, but one of them made the mistake of shouting out 'Hurrah for the sailors' and was flogged on the spot for his outburst. The rebelling seamen were put in irons in part of the ship where they could not converse with the convicts, doubtless in case they incited them to take over the ship. The remainder of the voyage was navigated by the officers, some of the seamen who agreed to return to duty, some of the soldiers and occasionally a few of the convicts.

Surgeon Galloway kept a journal of the *Isabella*'s voyage, in which he describes conditions on board. He recorded that the diseases occurring on the first part of the voyage were those associated with seasickness. However, with a change in the weather after the Cape of Good Hope, when dense fogs predominated, illnesses became more severe and difficult to cure. Significantly, he highlighted the fact that those convicts who had come from the *Captivity* made up the bulk of the sick convicts. This he attributed to an outbreak of fever on the prison hulk before they left. The significance of his comment can be found in an official Australian document. The document is the New South Wales convict death register, which records that Job Nobbs's life sentence was a short one. He died just four months after landing on Australian soil, in July 1832. Perhaps the voyage was just too much for him.

---

229 Thomas Galloway (*c.* 1780–1852) was appointed Royal Navy surgeon in 1801 and served on several convict ships. He was also surgeon on a number of immigrant ships, including the *Margaret*, on which there were forty deaths during a voyage in 1841. An inquiry exonerated him.

Power to the People

On Tuesday 5 October 1802 Daniel Kennedy, a sailor in His Majesty's navy, was the subject of a court martial. His crime was that, with others, he had taken the ship *HMS Albanaise* to Malaga and handed it over to the French.[230] One of the twelve officers who found him guilty and condemned him to be hanged was 30-year-old Captain George Wolfe, who was unaware that in under a year he would also find himself facing a possible death sentence.

On Christmas Day 1802 Wolfe took charge of a new ship, the frigate *L'Aigle*, which had been captured from the French, and in March 1803 he was given orders to repair to Portland to impress men into the navy and recruit volunteers. All men aged between 18 and 55 experienced in seamanship, except fishermen, were liable to be impressed. On 1 April he dropped anchor in Portland Roads.[231] His first action was to go to Weymouth to obtain a warrant from Samuel Weston, the mayor of that town. But Weston's signature bore little weight on the Isle of Portland where he had no authority.

Before dawn the next morning the captain, accompanied by Lieutenant Francis Hastings, Lieutenant Jefferies of the marines, and about fifty sailors and marines landed at Castleton beach on the north of the Isle of Portland. As far as Portlanders were concerned, they had no right to be there. Ever since the tenth century the islanders had paid a local tax, called Quit Rent, which in their mind excluded them from compulsory recruitment into the armed forces. The story of what happened next varies, depending on which report you read. In any event the locals decided to take matters into their own hands. One version is that as soon as the press gang landed they were fired upon by a number of sailors collected on the beach, accompanied by others; a scuffle then ensued, and two of the rioters, named Porter and Wey, were secured, the one armed with a poker, the other with a reap-hook. The remainder of the mob then retired to Easton where they were re-enforced by nearly 300 men armed with muskets, pistols and cutlasses, which had been plundered from Admiral Christian's military transport ships, wrecked seven years earlier.

The story continues that this formidable body of islanders, urged on by two constables, lost no time in attacking their unwelcome visitors, sixteen

---

230   The French built *Albanaise*, which was captured by the British in 1800 and taken into service by the British navy. In 1800 the crew mutinied and the ship was taken to Malaga and handed back over to the French.
231   A deep-sea anchorage off Portland.

or seventeen of whom were dreadfully wounded. At some point the marines opened fire, killing four of the crowd and causing them to retreat. Another account of events was contained in a letter sent to the editor of the *Cheshire Courant*,[232] setting out the facts as they came out in the subsequent trial. According to the letter, when Wolfe and his men landed they made their way to Chiswell, where they impressed Henry Wiggatt and Nicholas Way, after battering his door down. An alarm soon spread around the island and a large group assembled around the Great Pool at Easton. Moving towards Easton, Wolfe was challenged by Zachariah White, Chief Constable of the island's Court Leet, who claimed that because their warrant was not signed by a magistrate it was null and void and implored them to withdraw. Taking no notice, the press gang moved into Easton Square at about 6.30 am, where they were confronted by the crowd. Wolfe grabbed a man by the collar and when he pulled away Wolfe fired his pistol, which signaled the marines to start shooting. Three men were killed: Richard Flann and Alex Andrews, both quarrymen, and Richard Lano, a blacksmith who was standing by the entrance to his workshop. Richard Bennett and Mary Way, Nicholas Way's sister, were both wounded, Mary fatally, by a bullet in her back. In the affray the marines did not go unscathed; ten of them were injured, nine to the extent that they had to leave the navy.

The subsequent inquest found that the deceased had been murdered and as a result Wolfe, Hastings and Jefferies were committed for trial at the assize court. Midshipman John Morgan was also arrested for the crime but was not tried. On the day of the trial, 29 August, the court was packed, and the three accused looked spectacular standing in the dock in full uniform. Central to the prosecution's case was that the impress was illegal, bearing in mind especially that a magistrate had not signed the warrant and Portlanders were exempt anyway. The judge dismissed this argument, asserting that the impressment was legal, even on Portland. Defending the actions of the press gang Wolfe said that he was acting in self defence when he fired his gun. Although the trial lasted six hours it took the jury just a few minutes to decide that the parties were not guilty of murder and had simply been doing their job.

After the trial, an interesting though unsubstantiated postscript emerged. It appears that the coroner who conducted the inquest was also a lawyer, and having found the press men guilty of murder went on board the *L'Aigle* after the inquest and begged Captain Wolfe to employ him in drawing up

---

232   *Cheshire Courant* 19/4/1803.

affidavits in their defence, claiming, at the same time, that the murder verdict was given in consequence of his dreading the resentment of the population of Portland. Many of the contemporary newspapers described the Portland affair as a riot, but to the people of Portland and many others it was slaughter, a fact finally recognised by the navy in 1978, when a rear admiral unveiled a plaque to the memory of the islanders 'who were shot by the press gang during its unlawful raid on the Royal Manor of Portland in what was known as the Easton Massacre.'

> To the memory of the following islanders
> who were shot by the Press Gang,
> during its unlawful raid on the Royal Manor of Portland
> in what was known as the Easton Massacre,
> on April 2nd. 1803:
> Alexander Andrews, quarryman,
> Richard Flann, quarryman,
> William Lano, blacksmith,
> and Mary Way who died later of
> wounds received in the same raid.
> This plaque was unveiled by
> Rear Admiral G. I. Pritchard on April 23rd.1978
> Masons { B. H. Otter / C. A. Durston }

Memorial erected in St George's church, Reforne, to commemorate the Easton Massacre. (Author copyright.)

***

During the Napoleonic Wars[233] it had not been possible to import corn into the country and in accordance with the laws of supply and demand the prices of home-grown wheat rose, providing large profits for farmers and landowners. As the conflict came to an end, in 1815, landowners feared that their profits would be reduced and so put pressure on the government to keep the prices high artificially. The result was the Corn Law Act of 1815, which severely limited the import of cheap corn by putting a tariff on it, consequently keeping the price of bread high. Bread, of course, was the

---

233   1803–1815.

stable diet of the poor and the act was not popular among them, but because Parliament was dominated by the landowning class the populace was powerless, and resorted to taking matters into their own hands. On 6 March 1815 a large riot took place outside Westminster requiring the intervention of the military.

Despite wide and continued opposition to the Corn Laws after they had been passed, they remained, and the price of a loaf continued to rise. In its 18 May 1816 edition the *Royal Cornwall Gazette* gave the latest cereal prices, informing its readers that 'Wheat rose on Monday morning, at Mark Lane,[234] six shillings a quarter, making with the rise last Friday, ten shillings beyond last Monday's prices. Flour rose ten shillings the sack.' It then went on to say that 'the previous Monday morning, as a consequence of the advance in the price of bread, several groups of the manufacturing poor assembled at different parts of Bridport, complaining of the grievance, added to their want of employment from the present stagnation of trade'.[235]

Mr Edward Nicholas, a Bridport lawyer, was there on that Monday and described what happened. About 1 o'clock in the afternoon he saw several hundred persons gathered in West Street. In the midst of them there was a brewer's dray cart with several casks on it. The crowd was acting in a riotous way and among the shouting and bawling he heard glass breaking. About half a dozen, who were mostly men, were sitting astride the horse and one, Jacob Powell, was sitting on one of the barrels, holding a staff aloft with a loaf of bread on it. The casks of beer and the dray had been taken from the brewery of Samuel Gundry. The

Food riots took place in reaction to the rising cost of bread. (Courtesy of the American Library of Congress Collection.)

---

234   Home of the London Corn Exchange.
235   *Royal Cornwall Gazette* 18/5/1816.

sound of broken glass came from windows of the shops of bakers, who as far as the protesters were concerned were making excess profits at the cost of the poor. After an hour or so the magistrates read the riot act before the mob, but they were ignored. So, Edward Nicholas decided to take matters into his own hands. He offered, if ten men would join him, to go among the crowd and secure the ringleaders, and without further ado he did just that, forcing his way through to the dray and dragging off Jacob Powell. Eventually, the crowd was disbursed and several of the rioters were arrested and put before the magistrates.

Of the seven who were committed, five appeared at the July assizes. Before and after the Crown case was put to the jury each of the accused was given an opportunity to defend himself. Jacob Powell, a wool-comber and the eldest of the prisoners, aged 31, claimed that he came upon the dray and saw a woman fall from it. He immediately went to her aid to stop it going over her and when he stooped down the crowd overcame him. He then jumped on the dray to avoid being injured. He denied carrying a staff with a loaf on it. Twenty-two-year-old Hannah Powell, Jacob's sister, admitted that she was in the town but broke no windows. The youngest of those in the dock was blacksmith William Fry, aged 16, who faced the additional and more serious charge of stealing beer from Gundry's. Samuel Follett also faced an additional charge to that of rioting, as he had been recognised breaking the windows of the house and shop of John Fowler, a baker. It took the jury just a few minutes to find all the prisoners guilty. Elizabeth Phillips, who had been identified as being at the head of the mob going towards the brewery, was much affected by the trial, received her sentence of three months' imprisonment with her baby in her arms. The remainder were given terms ranging from six to twelve months with hard labour.

The case against the Bridport rioters was held before Justice Park, who made very clear before the trial, when addressing the grand jury, exactly what he thought of the whole affair. His actual words give an interesting insight into a view of the poor and their situation held by many at the time. He said:

'It appeared that this riot had been committed merely because those deluded persons imagined they should be able to redress certain grievances under which they laboured; but it was much to be lamented that they should think such a measure could add to their comforts .... The magistrates did not bear the sword in vain. The grand jury would have to teach them this fearful lesson; and when they retired to their private residences, it would be necessary to inform their less enlightened neighbours, that all attempts of this kind only increase the evil; it was one of those things, the end whereof was death. There was no occasion to plead poverty for the purposes of crime; charity was never withheld from the honest and industrious, but measures of this nature hardened the hearts of the charitable; and it was only to be wished that the deluded part of mankind would take warning by these cases.'

He went on to make a clear reference to those persons who were championing political and social change on the national scene when he completed his oration by commenting that 'there were persons of that nefarious character among us who turned a temporary pressure into a belief that it would be permanent. Such persons were enemies of good order and peace of society and should be avoided by the poor and illiterate.'[236]

Twenty-seven years later in the same court, another judge, Justice Atcherly, had another message for a grand jury, which was made up largely from the county's gentry. He said:

'In addressing gentlemen of your station and education, I need hardly say that it is the truest policy to provide for the wants, the necessities, and the comforts of those who are called the lower orders. Gentlemen, if we wish to make the labourer honest, we must find him the means of obtaining an honest livelihood; if we wish to make him peaceable and quiet, we must attract him, not by terms of severe contract, but by those acts which will convince him that those above him are not tyrants and oppressors, but protectors and his friends; if we wish to fortify his moral principles, the true way to do so is by holding out to him the opportunity of obtaining education and knowledge of every kind, and above all a knowledge of religious comfort. I would only say it is by thus binding together the different classes of society that we will best protect private property – shall best maintain public peace – best cement the different parties of society, and produce that state of things that no subtlety of penal enactment can ensure.'[237]

One can only imagine what the twenty-three members of the grand jury thought of this advice.

Similar sentiments to those of Atcherly were expressed five years earlier in part of an article that appeared in the 1 November 1838 edition of the *Chronicle*. Addressing farmers and landowners, it advised them to 'treat your labourers well; give them fair wages; bind them to you by kindness and an affable demeanour'. There was also a message to the Dorset labouring classes.

236   *London Times* 7/8/1816.
237   *Sherborne Mercury* 11/3/1843.

It had come to the paper's attention that the organisation of labour, which had started elsewhere, was extending into the county, something which it regretted, and advised the labouring class to ignore those who claimed that by combining together they could improve their lot, because their real motives were to encourage discontent, encourage them into lawlessness and disturb the tranquility of the country. The reference to workers combining to improve their lot had particular significance in the county of Dorset. Four years previously a trial took place in Dorchester that had national repercussions, and today is recognised as a seminal moment in the social history of our country.

***

In the history of the Dorset assizes there are two trials that stand out above all others. The first is the Bloody Assizes, at which, in 1685, followers of the Duke of Monmouth who attempted to usurp King James II were tried for treason. The second is that of six agricultural labourers in 1834.

The story of the six agricultural labourers, who came to be known as the Tolpuddle Martyrs, begins in the small village of Tolpuddle, situated eight miles east of Dorchester. Among its inhabitants was George Loveless, with his wife and three children. George earned his living as a master ploughman on the farms of James Northover and spent much of his spare time preaching the Methodist gospel in the local area. George's brother James also worked for Northover and like his brother could read and write and was an active Methodist.

In the early 1830s there was a general attempt by agricultural workers to increase their wages. George Loveless recalled, in 1873, that the men in his parish met with their employers and an agreement was reached that their masters would pay them as much as others in their district, ten shillings a week. But the employers around Tolpuddle reneged and would only allow nine shillings and within a few months the amount was reduced to eight. As one can imagine, the workers were dissatisfied with this, so appealed to the local magistrate, William Morton Pitt, for help. Pitt told them that if two or three of them went to County Hall in Dorchester he would call upon the chief magistrate and the employers to meet them there the following Saturday. George was the man appointed as the spokesperson for the Tolpuddle workers, but the meeting, as far as he was concerned, was most unsatisfactory. He was told that labourers must work for what their employers thought fit to pay them and that there was no set rate that masters were required to pay their servants. Another person present at the meeting was the vicar of Tolpuddle who was also at the first meeting with the employers and had assured George and the others that as a witness to what was agreed he would ensure that the employers would carry out their promise to pay ten shillings. Now, he denied that he had said anything of the sort. Naturally, this angered the men from Tolpuddle, who felt betrayed, and the following evening several windows in the rectory were smashed.

The workers returned to their homes after their trip to Dorchester empty handed but were not going to let the matter rest. George sent a message around the village inviting the men to a meeting on the village green. About fifty persons turned up and he suggested that they should unite to argue their case for receiving the same wage that others in the area were receiving. He told them that he had heard of trade associations that had been set up to increase the bargaining power of workers and that he would make enquiries and then call another meeting. George wrote to Robert Owen, leader of the Grand National Consolidated Trade Union (GNCTU), resulting in two members of a trade society arriving in the village, who helped them set up a friendly society.

News about the goings on in Tolpuddle got around and one man who took a particular interest was James Frampton of Moreton, who had been present at the meeting in Dorchester. On other occasions he had taken an active part in confronting agricultural workers and their families, at Bere Regis and Winfrith, who were demanding higher wages. Moreover, he had been in France at the time of the French Revolution and seen the results of bloody insurrection. Determined to nip in the bud any sign of workers organising themselves, he sent John Lock, son of his head gardener, to spy on the Tolpuddle men who were meeting regularly. The society had its own rules and men who wished to join were required to go through a ceremony, which included the use of an image of a skeleton, prayers and swearing allegiance. Unfortunately for Frampton, nothing the men were doing was illegal,[238] so he wrote to the Home Secretary, Lord Melbourne, expressing his concerns and asking for help to find a way of prosecuting the ringleaders. Melbourne came up with the Incitement to Mutiny Act of 1797,[239] part of which made it an offence to swear a secret and illegal oath. At daybreak on 24 February

238 Trade unions had been legal since 1824.
239 The Incitement to Mutiny Act was passed after the Spithead and Nore mutinies and was aimed at preventing the persuasion of sailors or soldiers to commit mutiny.

1834 the village constable walked down Tolpuddle's main street, knocked on six doors and read six arrest warrants. The men he took into custody were George Loveless and his brother James, father and son Thomas and John Standfield, James Brine and James Hammett. The men were marched to the house of Charles Wollaston, chairman of the county quarter sessions and half-brother to James Frampton, in Dorchester, where they were questioned before being taken to Dorchester gaol.

The trial of the prisoners was set for the Lent assizes of 1834 and for the judge, Justice Baron John Williams, it was to be his first. On the day in question his initial task was to address the grand jury, which included among its members James Frampton and his son, Charles Wollaston and William Ponsonby, brother-in-law to Lord Melbourne. In his words to them the judge made plain his views on the charge. He told them that under the Incitement to Mutiny Act the taking of a secret oath was itself a crime and did not have to be for a seditious or illegal purpose, and that taking such an oath undermined the sacred oath which upheld the justice system. Moreover, openness and publicity had always been considered the criteria of honesty, implying that secrecy was equated with dishonesty. The grand jury found that there was a true bill to be answered by the six men and later in the day they were brought up from the court cells to hear the case against them. Edward Gambier, soon to be Sir Edward Gambier, led for the Crown and opened his case by referring the jury to the Act under which the prisoners had been charged, and to which they had all pleaded not guilty. He pointed out that a combination or confederacy of persons was unlawful if it imposed any oath not required or authorised by law, and then called witnesses to support the prosecution.

First in the witness box was John Lock, Frampton's spy, who described what happened to him one evening when he went to the house of Thomas Standfield, accompanied by four other labourers. He said that he was taken into a room where John Standfield was standing and noticed that the Loveless brothers were in the passage. The five men were then blindfolded and led into another room where a paper was read to them, although he could not remember what was said. Then they were asked to kneel and something else was read to them. Again, Lock could not recall what was read but he thought it was something from the bible. Having got up and taken off the blindfold Lock recalled seeing a large picture in the corner of the room resembling a skeleton. It was then that James Loveless said, 'Remember your end'. The men were then required to go through the same procedure again, of being blindfolded and kneeling, whilst further words were read to them.

Lastly, they had to kiss a book. This time, after removing his blindfold Lock observed that all the prisoners were present in the room and noticed that James Loveless was wearing something resembling a surplice. The rules of the Society were then read out, and something was said about having to pay a shilling on entering and then a penny a week, to support the men who were out of work.

Next to give evidence was Edward Legg, a farm labourer from Affpuddle, who corroborated the evidence given by Lock. He was equally forgetful about what was said to him at the time, although he did remember being told that the men were going to strike, and also something about souls being plunged into eternity if he did not keep the secret. Finally, cross-examined by Mr Burt, for the defence, he told the court that he knew all the prisoners personally; that they were all hard-working men and he had never heard a word against them.

When Mr Burt, defending James Hammett, John Standfield and James Brine, opened his case, he too, like the prosecution, referred to the Mutiny Act, arguing that this piece of legislation had been framed for the protection of sailors at a time of great danger and surely did not apply to his clients. Mr Derbyshire, defending the Lovelesses and Thomas Standfield, told the jury that to satisfy the Act it was necessary to prove two things before the indictment could be sustained. That the prisoners had entered into an illegal association and that in pursuance of achieving its aims they had administered or taken an oath binding them to concealing unlawful acts. In respect of the oaths, he argued that they only had the evidence of two stupid witnesses who had chosen voluntarily to be blindfolded, listened to words they had largely forgotten, and could not recognise who uttered them. Regarding the legality of the society, Derbyshire argued that its purpose was to provide a fund for the needs of its members and their families, if they were thrown out of work. The prisoners acted in a spirit of prudential foresight not sedition and civil unrest. After the evidence had been given and the lawyers had made their submissions a letter was read from the defendants stating that if they had done anything in violation of the Act of Parliament, it was quite unintentional. All that they intended in creating the society was mutual protection.

The men in the dock did not have to wait long for the jury to make a decision that would change their lives forever. After five minutes of deliberation a verdict of guilty was pronounced on all six. But if the verdict was swift the punishment was not. It was thirty-six agonising hours before the men were brought back to the Crown Court to hear their fate. Addressing them, Judge

Williams referred to their plea that they had no intention of doing harm, but he dismissed this and said that the intention of legal punishment was not just to penalise offenders but also to act as a warning and deterrent to others, and that was the nature of this case. Accordingly, he felt he had no discretion in the matter and sentenced each of the men to the maximum penalty under the law, seven years transportation.

Six men who a month ago had been sitting at home with their families were now bound for a foreign land and a very uncertain future. On 25 March, eleven days after the trial, they were taken by coach from Dorchester to Portsmouth, having had little time to say farewell to their loved ones. Waiting for them at the end of their journey was the prison hulk *York*,[240] which would serve as a temporary home until their departure to Australia. It was three weeks later that the convict ship *Surrey* set sail minus one of the six, George Loveless, who was taken ill and it was decided to hold him back until his health improved. This short delay enabled him to write a letter to his wife Betsy before he joined 240 other convicts on the *William Metcalfe*, bound for Van Diemen's Land.

Had it been any other case heard in the rural county of Dorset, it would have been forgotten by the public after a few weeks. But this would turn out to be no ordinary case and nobody could have guessed the huge repercussions it would have. Immediately after the verdict was made public, up and down the country, newspaper articles appeared, some supporting the verdict and others vilifying the harshness of the sentence, and soon the case became a cause célèbre. At the initiation of the GNCTU, meetings were held throughout the land opposing the sentence, and on 21 April an estimated 100,000 people assembled and marched at Copenhagen Fields in London, resulting in a petition to the House of Commons requesting them to petition the King to suspend the sentences. In addition, the GNCTU had set up the London Central Dorchester Committee and sent out a plea for help in raising funds to support the men's families. *The Pioneer*,[241] a radical newspaper, was able to announce that funds were coming in from all parts of the country. If the men were to get a reprieve, time was of the essence. Once the ship had sailed it would be impossible for the men to be returned, but it would take many more petitions and debates in the House of Commons before the men were pardoned.

---

240   Launched in 1807, the *York* was a 74-gun ship of the line which served in the Napoleonic Wars. She was converted to a prison hulk in 1819 and was located at Gosport and London until 1848 when a serious rebellion broke out. Typically she confined about 500 convicts.

241   *The Pioneer* 12/4/1834.

The *Surrey* arrived in Sydney harbour on 17 August after a voyage of 129 days, and after remaining onboard for two weeks the men were sent to Hyde Park Barracks where they were assigned to their workplaces. John Standfield was detailed to work on the Bolwarra Estate, situated on the Hunter River and owned by Richard Jones.[242] John just had time to make a desperate farewell to his father before boarding the steamer *Sophia Jane* which would take him on the 150-mile journey. During his time at Bolwarra John was allowed to visit his father who was working as a shepherd on a farm just three miles away. On his first visit he found him in great distress and on the next he was covered in sores, all due to his terrible living conditions. Thomas was living in a tiny wooden hut, similar in size to a sentry box, open to the sky and infested with blowflies. John continued to visit his father for another nine months, until he was moved to another station.

In January 1836 the younger Standfield was approached by a constable and told he was going to a place named Newcastle, where he would join his father. After meeting him there the two of them embarked on a long miserable journey, during which they were unable to wash or change their clothes and were only fed occasionally. Ironically, their final resting place was where they had begun life in Australia, Hyde Park Barracks. To their surprise they were joined there by James Brine and James Loveless and the four of them joined a chain gang working on Sydney's roads. Then, one day, they were summoned to the principal superintendent's office. One wonders what their initial reactions were when, after nearly two years away from England, they were told that they would be granted a conditional pardon after they had served three years. It was not until September 1837 that they began their journey home, arriving in Plymouth the following March, four years to the month of their conviction.

But what of James Hammett and George Loveless? Hammett had been working for Richard Eyre[243], owner of an estate containing three thousand sheep, and heard of his pardon quite by chance. In May 1836 his boss had ridden out to give his shepherd new orders and whilst they were talking a newspaper fell from his bag. He picked it up and gave it to James, who, opening it up was astonished to see his name, and even more astonished to

---

242 Richard Jones was a whale fish merchant and sheep importer. He was also president of the Bank of New South Wales and member of the Legislative Council.

243 Richard Eyre (1815–1901) was a controversial character. He became an intrepid explorer of Australia and was made lieutenant governor of New Zealand and the Leeward Islands. He was then made governor of Jamaica. He became controversial when a revolt took place and during the repression more than 400 of the rebels were executed. Back in England some called for his trial as a murderer, but a grand jury declined to indict him.

find that he had been pardoned. He immediately went to Eyre and begged to be sent home and like the others he initially was sent to Hyde Park Barracks. Unfortunately, his journey home was interrupted when he was convicted of an assault and had eighteen months added to his sentence. He did not get home until September 1839. George Loveless's return home was also delayed but for a different reason. Before hearing of his pardon he had written to his wife, asking her to bring out the family to join him, and now he was not prepared to depart Van Diemen's Land until he was sure she had not already embarked on her own journey. He did not set foot on English soil until March 1838.

James Hammett was the only one of the six men to return to Tolpuddle. The other five were given farms near Chipping Ongar in Essex, before emigrating to Canada with their families a few years later. When they arrived there, they swore another oath not to tell anyone, including their children and grandchildren, anything about their convictions. This, in spite of all the immigrants who would have known about the trial, they somehow managed to do. Not until 1901, after they had all died, did word get out. It was in 1904 that the name Tolpuddle Martyrs was first mentioned and it lives on today in the annual festival held each year in July in the village of Tolpuddle.

This memorial stands in the grounds of the Tolpuddle Martyrs Museum, in Tolpuddle. It commemorates suffering of the six agricultural labourers who were transported to Australia. (Author copyright.)

Sources

Primary Sources

A Calendar of Prisoners Tried at the Assizes, Dorchester, Dorset. Dorset History Centre.

Convict Hulks, Convict Prisons and Convict Lunatic Asylums: Quarterly Returns of Prisoners. National Archives, HO8.

Dorset Assizes: Commitment and Bail Records. National Archives, HO27.

Dorset, England, Calendars of Prisoners, 1854–1904. Dorset History Centre.

Dorset, England, Church of England Baptisms, Marriages, and Burials, 1538–1812. Dorset History Centre.

Dorset, England, Church of England Births and Baptisms, 1813–1906. Dorset History Centre.

Dorset, England, Church of England Marriage, Banns, 1813–1921. Dorset History Centre.

Dorset, England, Dorchester Prison and Discharge Registers, 1782–1901. Dorset History Centre.

Dorset, England, Jury Lists, 1825–1921. Dorset History Centre.

Dorset, England, Poor Law and Church of England Parish Records, 1511–1997. Dorset History Centre.

England and Wales, Civil Registration of Births, Marriages and Deaths. General Register Office.

Home Office: Criminal Entry Books. Entry Books of out-letters, warrants and pardons, 1782–1871. National Archives, HO13.

Home Office Criminal Registers, England and Wales, 1805–1892. National Archives, HO27.

Millbank Prison Registers: Male Prisoners. National Archives, HO24.

Neill, Dr Alexander, Journal of the voyage of the *Recovery* in 1836. Royal Navy Medical Journals, 1817-1857. National Archives.

Pinney, Lady Hester. Letter to Thomas Hardy regarding the case of Martha Brown, dated 16/1/1926.

Portland Prison, Dorset, General Record of Prisoners (Record of Conduct During Imprisonment). National Archives, PCO M2.

Portland Prison, Dorset, Governor's Records. National Archives, PCO M2.

Quarterly Returns of Convicts in Fulham Refuge. National Archives, HO8.

Quarterly Returns of Convicts in Brixton Prison. National Archives, HO8.

Secondary Sources

Aldred, Guy (1912) *Richard Carlile: His Battle for the Free Press.* Bakunin Press.

Bateson, Charles (1974*) The Convict Ships,* 2nd edition. Brown, Son & Ferguson.

Bentley, David (1998) *English Criminal Justice in the Nineteenth Century.* Hambledon.

Campbell, Theophila (1899) *The Battle of the Press: As Told in the Story of the Life of Richard Carlile.* A. & H.B. Bonner.

Clifford, Naomi (2016), *The Disappearance of Maria Glenn, A True Life Regency Mystery.* Pen and Sword History.

Cutler, Rev. Richard (1865) *Original Notes of Dorchester and the Durotriges. Dorset Chronicle.*

Dixon, Thomas (2012) *The Tears of Mr Justice Willes.* Journal of Victorian Culture.

Filleul, Rev. S.E. (1911) *The History of the Dorchester Gallows.* Article in the DNHAS Proceedings. Vol. 32.

Finch, Henry (undated) *Lecture on Justice and Injustice in Early Nineteenth Century Dorset.* https://www.academia.edu/8637763/Justice_and_Injustice_in_Early_Nineteenth_Century_Dorset.

Guttridge, Roger (1986) *Dorset Murders.* Roy Gasson Associates.

Hutton, John (2017) *Portland Convict Prison, Miscellany.* Print Team (Dorset).

Mayo, Charles H. (1908) *The Municipal Records of the Borough of Dorchester.* William Pollard & Co.

Morris, Stuart (1985) *Portland: An Illustrated History.* The Dovecote Press.

Oxford Dictionary of National Biography (2020) Oxford University Press, https://www.oxforddnb.com/.

Pinney, Lady Hester (1966) *Thomas Hardy and the Birdsmoorgate Murder 1856.* Toucan Press.

Underdown, David (1992) *Fire from Heaven.* Harper Collins.

Wachsmann, Dr Nickolaus (2020) *Review of Oxford History of the Prison: The Practice of Punishment in Western Society.* www.reviews.history.ac.uk.

Whiteway, William (1991) *William Whiteway of Dorchester, His Diary 1618–1635.* Dorset Record Society.

Newspapers

The Atlas
Bell's Life in London and Sporting Chronicle
Bell's Weekly Messenger
Bridport News
Bury Post
Cheshire Observer and General Advertiser
Chester Courant and Anglo-Welsh Gazette
Daily Telegraph and Journal
Devizes and Wiltshire Gazette
Dorset County Chronicle and Somerset Gazette
Frome Times
The Globe
Gloucester Journal
Hampshire Chronicle
Hull Advertiser
Kentish Gazette
London Evening Mail
Morning Advertiser
New South Wales Gazette
The Pioneer

Poole and South-Western Herald
Potter's Electric News
Public Ledger
Queensland's Early Pioneers
Reading Mercury
Royal Cornwall Gazette
Salisbury and Winchester Journal
Southern Times
The Scotsman
Southampton Town and County Herald
The Standard
Taunton Courier
The Times
Warwickshire Advertiser
Western Daily Press
Western Gazette
Western Flying Post
Westmorland Gazette and Kendall Advertiser

Internet Sites

I have lost count of the number of internet sites I visited. Here are some of the main ones I used in my research.

Academia research papers: www.academia.edu
Ancestry: ancestry.co.uk
Capital punishment UK: www.capitalpunishmentuk.org
Closed Pubs: closedpubs.co.uk
Convicts of Australia: www.convictrecords.com.au
Dorset Ancestors: www.dorset-ancestors.com
Families Unearthed: familiesunearthed.com
Findmypast: findmypast.co.uk
Hansard online: www.hansard.parliament.uk
Internet Archive: Archive.org
JSTOR library of academic papers: www.jstor.org
National Library of Australia: www.nla.gov.au
New South Wales State Archives and Records: www.records.nsw.gov.au
Old Bailey online: www.oldbaileyonline.org
Parliamentary Archives: www.archives.parliament.uk
Prison History: www.prisonhistory.org
Smuggling UK: www.smuggling.co.uks
Van Diemens Land Founders and Survivors: www.digitalpanopticon.org
Victorian Children: www.victorianchildren.org
Victorian Crime and Punishment: www.vcp.e2bn.org

Index